# THE ART OF NON-CONFORMITY

### Set Your Own Rules, Live the Life You Want, and Change the World

## CHRIS GUILLEBEAU

TURNAROUND

First published in the US by Perigee, a member of the Penguin Group (USA) Inc.

PUBLISHER'S NOTE

While the author has made every effort to provide accurate telephone numbers and Internet addresses at the time of publication, neither the publisher nor the author assumes any responsibility for errors, or for changes that occur after publication. Further, the publisher does not have any control over and does not assume any responsibility for author or third-party Web sites or their content.

A CIP catalogue record for this book is available from the British Library.

ISBN 978-1-87326-276-4

*To Jolie, my partner in world domination and life*

**THE ROAD AHEAD**

car will not take me where I want to go in life." On leaping and the sudden appearance of nets. When next in Warsaw, make sure you have a ticket home from Tokyo.

## Conclusion: Dangerous Ideas

Changing the world is always practical. "Men wanted for Hazardous Journey." Code words for marginalization. The opposite of luck. What's *your* dangerous idea?

## PROLOGUE

When you were a kid and wanted to do something your parents or teachers didn't like, you may have heard the question "If everyone else jumped off a bridge, would you?" The idea is that it's not good to do something stupid, even if everyone else is doing it. The logic is, *Think for yourself instead of following the crowd.*

It's not bad advice, even if it's sometimes used to exert control more than to support independent thinking. But one day, you grow up and suddenly the tables are turned. People start expecting you to behave very much like they do. If you disagree and don't conform to their expectations, some of them get confused or irritated. It's almost as if they are asking: "Hey, everyone else is jumping off the bridge. Why aren't you?"

I wrote this book to help bring the childhood message up to adulthood application. Screw those people jumping off the bridge. Make your own decisions. Live your own life.

Asking "why?" to everything like a three-year-old is helpful in making sure you don't jump off the bridge without at least considering the alternatives. Whenever you find yourself confronted by a request, obligation, or expectation you don't like, it helps to look carefully for the motivations and rationale behind what you hear.

When you ask why and the answer comes back, "Because that's what you're supposed to do," you know you're looking out over the bridge again. In the average day, you'll confront this reality many times—in work, relationships, and the countless decisions and choices you are required to make. The presence of the bridge and the expectations of other people are somewhat unavoidable. Whether you jump or not, however, is entirely up to you.

Even if the people giving it to you weren't that great at following it themselves, the counsel you may have heard at a young age was correct. Why jump off the bridge just because everyone else is doing it? You can step back from the ledge, turn around, and walk away into new adventures that had previously been only fleeting ideas. You can also help other people walk away from the bridge, or you can rewrite the rules that brought you to the bridge in the first place. The possibilities are unlimited, but it all begins with the deliberate choice to think differently.

# PART I

# The Remarkable Life

It's your own life, so why not set your own rules? You can do good things for yourself while helping other people at the same time. This section will get you started.

# 1 Sleepwalkers and the Living World

Most men lead lives of quiet desperation and go to the grave with their song still in them.

—HENRY DAVID THOREAU

The purpose of this book is to transform your thinking about life and work. You'll benefit from the transformation if you're in a season of life where you're getting ready to make some changes. Alternatively, if you don't see any big decisions on the horizon but you'd like to create an opportunity for change, this will help too. Lastly, if you're feeling stuck in something and have always believed "there must be more to life," this book is for you.

As you set out on your journey, you'll meet a variety of people. Along the way some of them will help you, while others will stop at nothing to prevent you from succeeding. We'll look at how to connect with the people you need, and how you can help them while they're helping you. We'll also meet some of the people who set out to harm you—gatekeepers, critics, and vampires among others. I'll show you their agenda and their tactics—and how you can beat them.

You'll learn about world domination, creative self-employment, career independence, radical goal-setting, contrarian travel, and a number of other unconventional ideas. Some of these topics require lengthier study for full mastery, but this book is meant to be compact and complete. By reading and applying the lessons within, you'll be fully equipped to accomplish anything you set out to do. Hopefully, you'll also be *challenged* to do more than you ever thought possible before.

## Success, Motivation, and the $32,000 Lesson

In the battle between hope and fear, hope usually wins out in the end. Accordingly, this book is for people who want to change the world. I'm writing for believers, not cynics, and if you make some big changes as a result of the stories and ideas you read here, we will both have succeeded. In the event we succeed, you'll have the ability—and the obligation—to live life on your own terms and help other people while you're at it. The goal is simple: nothing will ever be the same.

If anything else results from our time together, I will have failed. In that case, I'll deserve one-star reviews on Amazon .com, and you'll deserve an apology for my wasting your time. I don't want one-star reviews, and no one likes to apologize, so I have the strong incentive to earn your trust and provide a rewarding experience.

After working in West Africa for four years as a volunteer aid worker, I returned to the United States to attend graduate school in the fall of 2006. The official story is that I completed a two-year master's degree in International Studies at the University of Washington. The real story is that I spent $32,000 to learn about motivations.

Later on we'll look at the overall experience of higher education in comparison to the formation of the writing career I began shortly thereafter. For now, the important point is that about halfway through checking off a list of required courses for graduate school, I realized that roughly 80 percent of the assignments I worked on had little or no value. The projects were simply "busywork" designed to keep students working on something so that the system could sustain itself.

I also noticed that this type of work was not conducted solely by students—faculty and administrators were also engaged in a significant amount of pandering. One professor who was wise to these strategies used the technical term "bullshit" to describe this kind of work. Bullshit is work that is done merely to complete requirements, make you look good, or otherwise fill up the hours of the day.

Just as faking it can be an effective way to get through higher education, mediocrity is the standard by which much work is judged once you get out of school. Assuming you've had some kind of job, you probably already know how this works. If you've ever completed a task for the sole purpose of making yourself look better without any improvement being produced for others (customers, colleagues, etc.), then you've been a participant in the game of mediocrity. Similarly, if you've ever been to pointless meetings that drag on far too long, this description should come as no surprise.

I'd like to keep the bullshit and the mediocrity to a minimum. It's a short book, and there's a lot to cover. In the 20 percent of the time that composed the rest of my graduate school experience, I learned an important lesson: "Always look carefully for someone's motivations and agenda." Whenever you read a book, for example, ask yourself, "Why did this person spend months or years crafting this material?" and "What is their agenda?"

Sometimes the agenda is stated; other times, it's hidden— but there is always an agenda. If you haven't learned this lesson before, congratulations, you are now $32,000 richer from having skipped graduate school. No need to thank me, but feel free to apply this lesson and start thinking about motivations and agenda whenever you read.

You also don't need to look for a hidden agenda here. I'm happy to save you some time and tell you up front why I wrote this book. My motivation is to help people challenge authority and live unconventional, remarkable lives. The mission is to support a full-scale revolution with a simple underlying message: *You don't have to live your life the way other people expect you to.*

If you stop reading now and begin living every day according to that statement, your life will never be the same. Since learning to think carefully about motivations is worth at least $32,000, I have no idea what learning to live life free from the demands of others is worth. You'll have to decide that for yourself. On the other hand, I hope you keep reading, since we do have a few other things to cover along the way.

## Important! I Do Not Want to Waste Your Time

Before we go any further, I want to make sure I don't waste your time. To make sure this book will be useful to you, I'm going to make a number of assumptions right here at the beginning. The assumptions are based on the following four principles:

- You Must Be Open to New Ideas

- You Must Be Dissatisfied with the Status Quo

- You Must Be Willing to Take Personal Responsibility

- You Must Be Willing to Work Hard

Most people who have fundamentally changed the world have done so through the use of all of these principles. Let's look at each of them in more detail before going on.

## 1. YOU MUST BE OPEN TO NEW IDEAS

I don't care if you are liberal or conservative, religious or agnostic, rich or poor, or any other category we are often grouped into by people who like to argue. In fact, I believe that many of these "either/or" descriptions are false dichotomies designed to set people against each other for no good reason. At best, they are irrelevant to our discussion, and for the most part, we're going to ignore them.

However, you must be open to new ideas. This does not mean you accept new ideas blindly—but rather, that you carefully consider something before dismissing it. Along with the new ideas, you'll need to question some of the old ideas you probably still have. Whether it's this book or any other resource, almost nothing you encounter will ever be 100 percent relevant to your situation. The goal is to focus on what *is* relevant and apply those key ideas to your life.

> I don't understand why people are frightened of new ideas. I'm frightened of the old ones.
>
> —JOHN CAGE

## 2. YOU MUST BE DISSATISFIED WITH THE STATUS QUO

You must have a desire to go above and beyond what you see around you. If you're happy with the way things are, I wish you the best—but this book will not help you. Over the next 200 pages I'm going to lead a full-frontal assault on the status quo. The status quo has its defenders and its passive majority who accept things the way they are; the audience for this book consists of people who are dissatisfied and ready for change.

To get an idea on what the status quo represents, take a look at the "11 Ways to Be Unremarkably Average" list below. This list and its variations represent a safe, comfortable life. The list is not complete, and you could probably add a few items to it based on your own experiences or those of other people you know.

## 11 WAYS TO BE UNREMARKABLY AVERAGE

1. Accept what people tell you at face value.
2. Don't question authority.
3. Go to college because you're supposed to, not because you want to learn something.
4. Go overseas once or twice in your life, to somewhere safe like England.
5. Don't try to learn another language; everyone else will eventually learn English.
6. Think about starting your own business, but never do it.
7. Think about writing a book, but never do it.
8. Get the largest mortgage you qualify for and spend 30 years paying for it.
9. Sit at a desk 40 hours a week for an average of 10 hours of productive work.
10. Don't stand out or draw attention to yourself.
11. Jump through hoops. Check off boxes.

Just as few people will criticize you for jumping off the bridge when everyone else is doing it, this kind of life insulates you from challenge and risk. It's also a life of quiet desperation that leaves you with a nagging question in the back of your brain: "Is this all there is? Did I miss something somewhere?" If you want something *different* from the life of quiet desperation, keep reading.

### 3. YOU MUST BE WILLING TO TAKE PERSONAL RESPONSIBILITY

You must take responsibility for what happens in your future, good or bad. Our past may be somewhat responsible for defining who we are at present, but it does not need to define our future. If you had a terrible childhood or someone deeply hurt you at some point in the past, here is your chance to prove them wrong. If you had a nurturing childhood and have never known deep hurt or social disadvantage, you're better off than the rest of us. Where much is given, much is required, so it's time to step it up.

Regardless of where you fall in that spectrum, from here on out, win or lose, you must be willing to take responsibility for yourself.

### 4. YOU MUST BE WILLING TO WORK HARD

Many people believe that the key to an improved lifestyle is *less work*. I think it's *better work*. I believe that most of us want to work hard, but we want to do the kind of work that energizes us and makes a positive impact on others. That kind of work is worth working for, and the other kind of work is worth letting go of, finished or not. Instead of being easy, the most memorable times in our lives are often the most challenging. Overcoming the challenge is worth it in the end, but the challenge itself is also worth pursuing.

* * *

If any of these principles sound basic to you, let me assure you that they are actually quite rare in application. Almost everyone says they are open-minded, but when it comes down to it, most of us are deeply uncomfortable with change. We like things the way they are, or at least the way we imagine them to be. Similarly, many people refuse to take personal responsibility for their lives. Instead, they look to others to meet their needs. When things go wrong, they blame external factors—their employer, their partner, their parents, the environment, the government—pretty much anyone other than themselves.

Most people accept the status quo without question, sleepwalking through life, looking in from the outside. When other people manage to escape, sleepwalkers find ways to marginalize or ignore them by pointing out something wrong with their escape plan. Finally, when it comes to work, many people put in long hours without actually working very hard. Their eye is on a future that is years or decades away. The mentality we'll look at here is all about working hard on meaningful work that matters both now *and* for the future.

Don't believe these things? No problem. I'm not offended and I hope you aren't either. For the sake of your time and my book reviews, though, I'm afraid that we aren't a good match, and your time will be better spent elsewhere. If you agree so far, or at least if you're willing to give it a fair shot, I invite you to join me for the rest of the journey.

A final warning before we continue: dangerous consequences can result from careful consideration of these ideas. People have quit their jobs, changed careers, founded charities, traveled to the far reaches of the earth, gone back to school or quit school entirely, and made all kinds of other unconventional changes to their lives as a result of thinking carefully about motivations. I'll tell you many of the stories as we go along, but I should first begin by telling you how all of this came about.

## Who Am I to Tell You All This?

Let's be very clear about something: I adhere to a guru-free philosophy, and I don't claim to have all the answers. What I have done, for better or worse, is chosen freedom as my highest personal value and learned to construct a life around that choice.

In a story that will be recounted further in chapter 6, I skipped high school and went to college instead. I met my wife while we were both earning our degrees. Jolie was also interested in living overseas and pursuing a different career path than the people around us were choosing. More than 10 years later, we're still together.

My last conventional job was at the age of 20, when I worked the night shift slinging boxes at FedEx in Memphis, Tennessee. The job sucked. One day I came home at 4 a.m. (if you stayed past midnight, you got 50 cents more an hour), and sat down at the table I had snagged for $15 from the Salvation Army. I looked around the room and thought, "You know, I don't think I want to do this anymore."

On a whim, I decided to check out a new website called eBay .com. Surveying my apartment for a bunch of old stuff I didn't need, I took a few photos of the items and decided to see if anyone was interested. This was in the early days of digital photography, so the process was old-school. I took the photos with a 35mm camera, dropped the film off at the drugstore, picked up the prints the next day, took the prints to the university library, scanned the images, and emailed them to my 15-year-old brother in Montana. Ken, my brother, had his own website that presented a critical analysis of anime films. Clearing some space on the server, he kindly uploaded my random images so I could use them in the auction listing.

My first week I made $19 an hour, which was more than twice as much as I made at FedEx. The same day the auction sales went through, I was scheduled to return to work after a three-day weekend. It was December, and Memphis was suffering a rare ice storm that left much of the city incapacitated. Ice storm or not, life at FedEx went on, so I prepared to pull out of the apartment driveway. Despite the needs of busy retailers during the holiday season, my car felt otherwise: as I began to back up, the car slid under the ice, lost control, and narrowly missed crashing into the parked truck belonging to my neighbor. "Why am I doing this?" I asked myself. I turned the engine off, went back inside, and never returned to the world of traditional work.

I quickly ran out of stuff to sell from around my house, so I started looking for wholesale sources. I found a good deal on Jamaican coffee—I could buy it for $10 a pound and sell it for $17 to connoisseurs in the United States—so I started receiving

50-pound sacks of beans at my apartment every week. In what became known as the great coffee disaster of 1999, one day the Salvation Army table collapsed under the weight of 80 bags of freshly ground inventory. The table crash freaked out the cat, and a semi-permanent layer of coffee dust settled on my floor, but I wasn't too worried about the damage. By that point I was able to invest in a superior table for $40 at Home Depot.

In addition to coffee, I learned about how to design websites and build an email list of potential buyers. For the next couple of years, I supported myself through a montage of creative self-employment. It wasn't making me a millionaire and it definitely wasn't strategic, but it worked. I had been an amateur musician for several years by then, and I started playing around town more frequently. I worked in the mornings, spent a couple of hours each afternoon studying jazz and music theory, played freelance gigs at night, and traveled to local festivals on the weekends.

Those things were fun. I enjoyed playing music, and I appreciated that I could work whenever I wanted. Something was missing, though—I felt like I was doing a lot of fun things, but I had no overall focal point for my life. I volunteered at my church and gave money to charity, but those acts seemed basic and insufficient compared to the urgent needs around the world. Depressed after 9/11 and browsing the Internet, looking for extended service opportunities, I read about a surgeon in Africa who had lived in war zones for 17 years and counting.

The story was fascinating. Many doctors and other professionals occasionally hop off for short stints abroad, but here was a guy who had chosen to spend nearly all of his working life in the poorest countries in the world. When I learned that he was living on board a hospital ship that was seeking long-term volunteers, I was hooked.

Together with Jolie, who was working as a high-school teacher at that point, I signed up for a two-year commitment that turned into four. The job and lifestyle were both extremely transformative. I worked with refugees, warlords, and presidents, and bounced around West Africa as I negotiated on behalf of the medical charity that operated the ship. Even though I worked for free, it was the best job in the world, and served as a better foundation than any university could have been.

The time to leave the best job in the world is right before you get tired of it. With the notable exception of Gary Parker, the surgeon I had first read about, many of the people I knew who continued to work in post-conflict countries year after year became bitter and cynical about their surroundings. I don't necessarily blame them for it—war zones are hard places to work—but I knew I didn't want that to happen to me. After four years, I was getting tired, and I didn't want to join the ranks of the cynical.

Jolie and I returned to the United States and began a new life in Seattle, Washington. I entered graduate school, worked full-time in a new publishing business and traveled to 20 countries a year while training for marathons on the side. My time in Africa had given me some good leadership experience, so I used those skills to volunteer at a local non-profit organization, where I served as the president of the board.

I kept busy, in other words, but once again I felt like something was missing. I wasn't sure what I was looking for, but I knew it was out there somewhere. I always loved to visit new places, and the years spent in Africa had helped me get comfortable with challenging travel situations. I decided to visit every country in the world, a quest that has taken me to more than 100 countries so far. Then I started writing about it, first on a website that grew to tens of thousands of regular readers, and now in the book that you are holding.

My story is not complete, and I certainly don't know it all. An important part of the guru-free philosophy is that no one is better than anyone else, and most of what you need to know, you already know—we're just going to fill it out a little. If you're just starting on your own unconventional journey, the best way to understand it is to talk about monkeys.

## The Five Monkeys and the Clear Alternative

Have you heard the story of the five monkeys in a cage? It goes like this. Five monkeys are thrown in a cage by a sadistic monkey-hater. Enough food and water is available at the bottom of the cage, saving them from starvation while forcing them to lead a boring life of staring through the glass every day. The food at the bottom is bad, but sufficient. At the top of the cage, however, a large stalk of bananas alluringly waits. Conveniently, a ladder to the top has been provided by the sadist.

After getting over the shock of being caged, one of the monkeys scales the ladder and reaches for a banana. All of a sudden a fire hose appears from nowhere. The monkey at the top of the ladder is soaked with cold water, but not only him—all of the other monkeys are soaked as well, in an exercise of group punishment for the sins of one freedom-loving monkey.

Over the next few days the experience repeats itself several times. One monkey makes a run for the bananas, the whole troop of monkeys gets soaked, and pretty soon the group starts beating up any monkey brave enough to scale the ladder. The bananas are still at the top, but just out of reach. The monkeys reluctantly accept the fate of living a life without bananas.

Then one day the experiment changes. The sadist takes one monkey out of the cage and replaces him with another one. Not knowing the consequence of being doused with cold water, the new monkey immediately begins to scale the ladder in pursuit of a banana, the rest of the monkeys pull her down before she reaches the top, and the troop settles in again.

The next day another monkey is replaced, and then another, and the process repeats itself: the new monkey lunges for the bananas, gets pulled down, and adapts. After five days, no monkey from the original troop remains, and no monkey has ever been soaked with cold water—but every monkey knows they are not supposed to climb the ladder. One of the monkeys finally asks, "Hey, why can't we eat the bananas?" The others shrug their shoulders and say, "We're not sure—we just know we can't."

*   *   *

Just like the monkeys in a cage ignoring the bananas above them, the choice of an unremarkably average life represents a life of sleepwalking. I wish I could say it was a conspiracy, but it's not. No sadist has thrown us all into a cage. Instead, it's a contagious pattern of settling for what is "good enough." Oblivious to the world that surrounds us, the life of sleepwalking offers little risk and little reward. No one will ever fault sleepwalkers for their choice, including me. There's just one big problem: for those of us who long for a life of adventure, the life of sleepwalking sucks.

Fortunately, we don't have to be caged monkeys. We are free to climb the ladder, grab the bananas, and even escape from the cage. Have you ever heard about how it's easier to ask forgiveness than permission? This is completely true, but there's even more good news: there are very few things you need to ask forgiveness *or* permission for.

If you're stuck in the cage, it's time to smash the glass around you and crawl your way out. You don't need anyone's permission to climb the ladder, and you don't need to apologize for escaping. If the sleepwalking life is the "real world" of the unremarkably average, the clear alternative is the *living world* of adventure. Come join the living world; it's open to all who are willing to embrace life as the adventure it should be.

## Where We're Going

We're going to look at several challenging ideas throughout the book. The most important idea, explored throughout each chapter, is what I mentioned earlier—you don't have to live your life the way other people expect you to. I assure you that if this sounds simple, it is deceptively so. To fully enact it requires persistence, courage, and determination. On the bright side, however, many things that are frequently presented as prerequisites are actually quite unnecessary. Among other things, you don't need to be especially intelligent, popular, rich, or otherwise privileged. Those qualities, in fact, can sometimes be detrimental to getting what you really want.

> The tragedy of life is not so much what we suffer, but rather what we miss.
>
> —THOMAS CARLYLE

The first part of the book, "The Remarkable Life," is all about the underlying philosophy behind challenging authority and charting a path for yourself. We'll look at setting the terms of your life, overcoming the internal obstacles of fear and insecurity, and taking on the external obstacles of gatekeepers and critics.

The second part, "Reclaiming Work," is all about changing the way we think about how and where we spend most of our productive time. We'll look at deriving security from your own competence instead of an employer, recruiting and deploying your own "small army," and the important question of money—how much you need and how you can get it.

The third part, "The Power of Convergence," advances the conversation about life and work. We'll consider the practice of radical exclusion, the pursuit of abundance, contrarian travel opportunities, and creating a legacy no matter how old you are. The conclusion ties together the "dangerous ideas" we've explored throughout the book and helps you to consider developing your own.

In addition to the overriding values of personal freedom and service to others, a few other ideas form the outline of the book. Each of them is briefly described below.

## BY ITSELF, MONEY HAS NO VALUE

We need money to live in a modern world, and we should find a way to get what we need without harming anyone else. However, by itself, money has no value—the value is produced only when we exchange money for other things. The reason why this is important is because many people don't know how much money they really need to do the things they want. They often wildly overestimate or underestimate how much money they need to exchange for their desired life.

According to near-unanimous scientific research, pursuing wealth for wealth's sake won't get you very far. A certain amount of money produces happiness, and a bit more produces a bit more happiness, but beyond that, the correlation between money and life satisfaction is null. Therefore, we'll look at using money as a tool to get what you want, but not as a pursuit in itself.

## CHOOSING BETWEEN YOURSELF
## AND OTHERS IS THE WRONG CHOICE

You'll have to make some hard choices to break out of the cage, but thankfully, choosing between yourself and others isn't one of them. You can do good things for yourself and still make the world a better place for everyone else. In fact, the goal is to find as much convergence as possible between these values. Give yourself permission to dream, and then get to work planning.

As we'll see in the next chapter (and throughout the book), though, it's not all about you. Even though we don't have to compromise on our personal ambitions, most of us are not ultimately happy with a life that is completely self-centered. Instead, our lives become most meaningful when we combine our own desires with an active strategy to help other people at the same time.

### CHANGING THE WORLD IS NOT ALWAYS PRACTICAL

Every idea in this book is designed to be highly practical, and there is no classroom knowledge here. However, be aware that "being practical" can sometimes be code language used by critics to marginalize your choices of freedom. Never forget that changing the world is not always a practical endeavor. Throughout history, most people who have made fundamental shifts in science, humanities, or the arts have been frequently accused of being impractical. At various times it has been impractical to think that women are equal to men, that humans should not own other humans, that criminals should be rehabilitated instead of merely punished, and so on.

The same may be true with the choices you make. It's not always about taking the easy way out—breaking out of the cage can be harder than falling in line with the rest of the monkeys—but you'll usually have a choice.

## YOU CAN PLAN FOR THE FUTURE WITHOUT DEFERRING YOUR LIFE NOW

The concept of deferred gratification, or sacrificing now to save for the future, can be helpful in setting aside money in a retirement account for old age. It can also serve as an effective rationalization for life avoidance. If you're only thinking about a hypothetical future, you can put aside the nagging sense that you could be doing more with your life now.

There's nothing wrong with thinking ahead, but life does not begin at age 65. Planning for tomorrow is good, in other words, but it doesn't have to affect every decision you make today. This brings us to the final preparation for jumping into the rest of the book: a reminder that time is limited.

### Life Is Short (Don't Forget)

As a final note, don't waste time in taking action toward assuming control of your life. As a general rule, it's usually better to do something than *not* do it. This may not *always* be the case—if you're on the fence about robbing a bank to buy donuts, it might be good to think of another way to acquire the donuts—but speaking generally, we tend to regret what we haven't done more than what we have.

Similarly, most people don't begin to think about leaving a legacy until they reach the end of their lives. If you're fortunate enough to begin from any earlier point in life, start thinking about your legacy immediately. Then, immediately thereafter begin living your life with that vision in mind.

If you don't know where to start, it's helpful to begin thinking about motivations. What motivates you? Why did you pick up this book? How do you feel about what you've read so far? By the way, if this kind of thinking is new to you, don't worry— we're going to look at it in several different ways throughout each part of the book.

There's an old story about a shaman with a reputation for curing insomnia. A busy professional who can't sleep tracks him down deep in the jungle, and the shaman agrees to help. The shaman sends instructions, and two weeks later, the professional sends back word that he's been cured. "Thanks so much! I've been sleeping great!" the note reads. The shaman sends back his own reply: "No problem. Come back and see me whenever you're ready to wake up."

Remember, the purpose of our time together is to transform your thinking about life and work. If you've been going through life as a sleepwalker, it's time to wake up. The journey begins right now.

# 2 Setting the Terms of Your Unconventional Life

The people who get on in this world are the people
who get up and look for the circumstances they want,
and, if they can't find them, make them.

— GEORGE BERNARD SHAW

After working in New York at the same comfortable job for
eight years, Bernard Lopez suddenly quit, broke the lease he had
signed on a new apartment, withdrew all his retirement savings,
and set out to travel across the United States by bicycle. One of
the questions he heard over and over (after the initial reaction
of "Are you crazy?") was "Are you doing this to raise money for
charity?"

If Bernard had said yes, most people would have nodded
their heads, their curiosity at least partially satisfied. It's usually
acceptable, if not always completely understood, to do something unconventional when it benefits other people. But Bernard wasn't raising money for charity or riding his bike across
the country to raise awareness for anything. "No," he said truth-
fully when people asked. "I'm doing it for me."

The idea for the bike ride of undetermined length came to Bernard after a series of shocks. He had recently ended a seven-year relationship, and shortly after that painful separation, his father was killed in an accident. After reflecting on these events during a long walk one day, the idea came to him: "I should leave my life in New York behind and bike across America."

> The great pleasure in life is doing what people say you cannot do.
>
> —WALTER BAGEHOT

The idea wouldn't go away, and instead of putting it off, Bernard chose to embrace it fully. He dutifully gave notice at his work and apartment, bought a bike, and started riding with no certainty of what would happen after he was done with the long ride. The initial days were jarring, but after a while he settled into a routine built entirely around riding all day and finding a place to stay at night.

At the end of the trip, Bernard relocated to Chicago with a feeling of invincibility. He began a new career and continued to travel every summer. It is no exaggeration, he told the readers of the online journal he kept, that the bicycle trip "has forever changed my life as it allowed me to reach my full potential and discover the real me."*

---

* Bernard Lopez's journal of his cross-country bike can be found at BicycleTrek.com.

## Discovering What You Really Want

Throughout the book, we're going to look at how our lives are intimately connected with others, how some of those people are counting on you, and how you can improve the lives of others all over the world. But over the next few pages, we're not going to think about that at all. The first part of this chapter will focus on your own personal goals and desires.

I believe in helping other people, but I also believe in relentless individualism. I believe that the crazy dreams and big ideas we have when we are young can be more than just fantasies. No, in the end it is not all about you—but there is also nothing wrong with doing things entirely for yourself.

As for me, I enjoy running for hours by myself, listening to music and thinking about my projects and plans. I enjoy taking solo trips around the world, arriving in cities without an agenda or obligations to fulfill. Some people call this selfishness, but I tend to believe the answer is more complicated—without the energy I derive from being by myself, I know that I wouldn't be of much use to anyone else later on.

Your dreams and big ideas belong to no one but you, and you never need to apologize for or justify them to anyone. If you already know exactly what they are, great; you're halfway there. Most of us, however, find that we need to take some time to think about it, and that's what this section will help with.

Because we usually need some time to figure this out, I'd like to voice an opinion right from the beginning: when it comes down to it, most of us do not want to sit on the beach and take it easy every day for the rest of our lives. Some of us would get tired after only a few days; others might enjoy it for an extended period of weeks or months. But just as we wonder "Is that all there is?" about conventional careers or life paths, after the initial detox of sunbathing and margaritas, we'd be asking the same questions about beach life—or whatever our vision of fantasy land is.

A while back I was walking in an unfamiliar part of town, and I passed by a gas station advertising lottery tickets. For a moment I thought, wouldn't it be fun to buy a ticket and dream? Then I realized that for the most part, I already had the life I wanted. I felt like I was in the 90th percentile of happiness and fulfillment. Of course I wanted to go further, but I knew that a lottery ticket (even a winning one) wouldn't take me there.

Most of us have lottery fantasies from time to time. I don't think they're necessarily harmful; I just think there's a better alternative. The alternative is to write your own winning lottery ticket, not by the sudden accumulation of wealth but the gradual reduction to what you decide is essential for your life. That's my proposal: creating your own life isn't quite like winning the lottery. It's better.

Instead of fantasy land, most of us crave a life of adventure and personal growth. Joseph Campbell understood this years ago when he wrote about the meaning of life. "People say that what we're seeking is a meaning for life," he began before clarifying, "I don't think that's what we're really seeking. What we seek is an experience of being alive."

As part of the experience of being alive, I believe we're looking to find our place in the world. On a planet of seven billion people, where do we fit in? This is essentially the central question of life, and finding the answer begins with understanding what we really want.

## What Do You Really Want to Get Out of Life?

Let's bring this analogy to what I call "life planning" and look at some practical ways of figuring out what you really want.* It's kind of like planning a wedding, but more important. There's nothing wrong with planning for a big, meaningful day; I just think it's even better to plan for a big, meaningful life.

Life planning begins with an unfortunate fact: many people have no idea what they really want to do or accomplish over the course of their time on earth. Instead of moving toward a destination, they become mired in "life avoidance" by ambling around without a clear sense of objective or purpose.

This is not entirely their fault. Our formal systems of education do not devote much time to coaching young people in how to figure this out. Evaluations of our abilities and knowledge, which typically take the form of standardized tests, focus almost entirely on occupational planning instead of "big picture" ideas.

Since a lot of adults have not figured out what they really

---

* Others use the terms *lifestyle design* or *personal development* to describe similar concepts.

want, they naturally find it difficult to pass on the values of soul-searching to children. For their part, spiritual leaders offer answers to the deep questions of creation, mortality, and ethics, but typically give little guidance on how we should actually fill our days. Thus, the cycle continues.

At some point, though, we each have to take responsibility for ourselves even if no one ever taught us to think about what we want. The lack of understanding and self-awareness hurts us more than anyone else. It holds us back from greatness and keeps us living unremarkably average lives. To break out of the sleepwalking pattern, we have to define what we want and then find a way to make it happen.

Credit where credit is due: a few years back, I read the book *Wishcraft* by Barbara Sher. One of the things Barbara said in the beginning resonated with me for a long time: "Whatever your dreams are, start taking them very, very seriously." That time in my life was a period of intense self-reflection, and I realized that even though I had done a lot of fun things by then, I hadn't been taking my dreams very seriously. I resolved to start doing that right away, and my life has been radically different since.

If you need help, there are a few different ways of figuring out what you really want to get out of life. Feel free to use any of the three approaches outlined on the following pages, modify them in the way that suits you best, or do something completely different.

Whichever way you choose, make sure you have at least a general idea before going forward.

## 1. CREATING YOUR IDEAL WORLD

In this classic exercise, you write out your idealized, perfect day in great detail, beginning from what time you get up and what you have for breakfast all the way through what you do for each hour of the day and who you talk to. The more detail you can add to the plan, the better.

Then you begin to make plans to adjust your life to get closer to the perfect day you've imagined for yourself. If you take this exercise seriously, you'll learn a lot about yourself even if you don't make a lot of changes based on the information you acquire. You may even begin making more conscious decisions about how you spend your time and what you focus on. I do this exercise once a year, in December, and always end up making several improvements the next year.

(You can get a more detailed worksheet and free MP3 audio recording for this exercise in the "Online Resources" section of this book.)

As I said, this exercise is a classic of the life-planning literature, and it can help if you've never thought much about what you really enjoy doing. There are two major weaknesses of this exercise, however, and if you don't compensate for each of them, you'll make significant improvements in your life, but you'll still find yourself wondering, "Is that all there is?"

The first weakness is that in the end, it's not all about you. You have to do more than create an ideal world for yourself, because most people really don't want to spend every day in a castle with someone bringing their toast to them in the mornings;

they want to do something meaningful with their talents. We'll come back to this concept in a moment, but since I promised you the first part was more about your own goals, let's keep it on hold for now.

The second problem is what this whole book is about—achieving big goals and living a remarkable life. How does that fit in? The ideal world exercise, for the most part, doesn't touch on goals at all. You define what kind of work you do, how you exercise, and so on, but what you are actually striving for is not included. Therefore, to focus on something meaningful that you work toward over time, you have to add some kind of goal-setting to the plan. I tend to think if something is worth doing, you might as well do it all the way—so I've added "radical goal-setting" to my own unconventional life planning.

## 2. RADICAL GOAL-SETTING

When you begin to think seriously about what you want to get out of life, the ideal world exercise helps with the structure. To complement the structure, however, you need a *focus*—and this is where the planning process I call "radical goal-setting" comes in. Radical goal-setting begins with a "life list" of things you'd like to do at some point in your life. A life list, also called a "bucket list," is composed of a long list of anything and everything you'd like to accomplish before you die.

There are numerous variations of these kinds of lists. Some have exactly 100 items, some have 30, some have an odd number.

To see examples of other people's ideas, go online and search for "life list"—but before you look at too many others, try to have some idea of what your own items are.

If you've never made your own list, it's a fun, eye-opening exercise. Spend an afternoon, or even just half an hour, listing out a range of activities and experiences you'd like to have sometime. If you have trouble getting started, this trick may help: fast-forward in your mind a long time (hopefully) to your death bed. When the time comes to say goodbye, what memories do you want to have? What would you regret if you hadn't done it? The ideas you get out of that kind of visualization are great candidates for entry on your life list.

The typical life list contains a wide variety of goals, ranging from the trivial ("try 100 fruits") to the difficult ("camp on Antarctica"). This kind of diversity is totally fine—it's your list, not anyone else's. However, one problem with having a wide range of goals is that a broad list can easily become fuzzy. What do you focus on at any particular time? Do you think about eating fruit or buying a sleeping bag for Antarctica? Therefore, to further refine the ideas, I like to take the overall list and break it down into measurable goals with an approximate deadline.

**One-Year Goals:** This list gets reviewed a few times a year, and I create next year's goals each December. I break this list down further into specific categories. Some of mine are *Writing, Health, Business, Friends, Family, Service, Travel, Income,* and *Giving*.

**Five-Year Goals:** This list gets reviewed once a year and contains some of the "big things" you hope to do in the near future. Note that as some of the goals on the one-year list are completed, other goals from the five-year list shift down.

**Lifetime Goals:** This list gets reviewed once a year and includes everything that you want to do, but either don't have a timeline for or will take a long time to accomplish.

By the way, make sure to include some really big ideas for your lifetime goals. The interesting thing about setting big goals is that once we get serious about planning for them, they tend to be achieved much more quickly than we initially expect. This is because we tend to overestimate what we can complete in a single day, and underestimate what we can complete over longer periods of time.

## 3. PLANNING FOR SERENDIPITY

I've always had a lot of projects going at once, and I enjoy the process of trying to keep all the plates spinning in the air. For me, if I'm *not* involved with a bunch of things simultaneously, I'm not happy. However, I also want to make sure I have time to embrace spontaneous ideas as well. We'll come to this later, but the point I want to make now is that a lot of people express surprise that I can do "so much."

I don't speak for all the organized people in the world, but I'm going to let you in on a secret that pertains to many of us:

# A FEW SUGGESTIONS (WHAT'S IN/WHAT'S OUT)

Far be it from me to tell you what your goals should be. It's your life, and you make the rules. Principles can be good starting points, however, so treat these ideas as suggestions for your consideration.

### What's In

- All the time you want for the people you love
- As much time as you need to think or plan
- Work that is fun, fulfilling, and challenging
- Some kind of financial independence (we'll look at this much more in chapter 8)
- A few "adventure" goals, like climbing Kilimanjaro or trekking through Nepal
- Some kind of travel goals, based on your own preferences (see chapter 10 for more info and ideas)
- Something that other people "don't get" but that makes perfect sense to you

### What's Out

- Drama and whiny people
- Busywork, or any work that ultimately lacks value
- Schedules that are set by other people
- Unnecessary obligations or things we do out of a sense of guilt

we're not as super-disciplined as you think. Really. What many of us have done instead is create a structure around our work that allows us to improvise. We *do* take the goals seriously and *do* work hard, but any discipline that comes about is usually a result of building a good structure to begin with.

Some of my most fulfilling experiences have been on days when I didn't have a lot planned. I've taken off for long runs in dozens of world cities without a map or any knowledge of the local language. I've watched the sunset without an agenda in Zambia and the Faeroe Islands. Almost every time I experience something like this, I always think to myself, "Wow. Life is good. I am so thankful to be alive."

Nor do the experiences have to be exotic to be serendipitous. I also enjoy sleeping in at home once in a while, going out for coffee in the afternoons, playing video games, and deciding on a whim to do something completely different one day.

Another way to think of it is this: in the long run, I want to be focused on the goals, my ideal world, and helping people however I can. In the short run, I have to take steps to ensure those things are happening, but it's not a highly regulated environment and I'm free to change it up whenever I want. If anything, it's a flexible-but-purposeful environment.

To anyone who says they don't like to set goals and prefer to take things as they come, I'd say, "Try setting the goals." I think you'll like seeing how much you can do when you really try. But don't worry, because you don't have to give up serendipity or flexibility. If anything, when you work toward getting what you really want, you'll have *more* time available to be spontaneous, and more energy for the "fun" things you like to do.

## You and the Rest of the World

As long as what you want does not cause harm to others, you never need to apologize for pursuing your own dreams and big ideas. They belong to you for a good reason. Once you've done some thinking about what you really want to get out of life, however, you'll likely *want* to move toward thinking about how you'll make the world a better place for others. This is because while you can do almost anything you want, in the end you probably won't be satisfied with a life that completely revolves around you.

Often this concept is presented as an afterthought. I've been to a number of seminars on entrepreneurship, and many of the talks have the same format: in a one-hour presentation, someone will spend 55 minutes talking about how to get rich. The final five minutes will consist of a reminder to "be sure and give back."

"This is what it's all about," the presenter sometimes says at this point, while the screen flashes photos of his trip to an orphanage on the other side of the world. Coming at the end of a long talk about making money, I've always thought of this slip as the "Oops!" moment. The Oops! is the forced moment when the realization hits that maybe there's more to life than what was shown during the main subject of the presentation.

To avoid the equivalent of the Oops! moment in your own life planning, start thinking seriously about how you will really change the world right from the beginning. These questions may help:

- What needs can you meet?

- Who looks to you as a leader?

- What bothers you about the world?

- How can you make things better?

- What can you offer the world that no one else can?

There's no need to wait to get serious about making a positive difference for those around you. As a general rule, if you don't know what to do on any given day, spend at least some of your time helping someone else. Instead of having this be an afterthought, you can build a life focused on the relentless pursuit of what you want coupled with the call to make a difference—starting today.

## Principles of Unconventional Living

When you reach the convergence between getting what you really want while also helping others in a unique way. I call this "world domination," where you live a life of adventure and focus on leaving a legacy that makes a radical difference for other people. There's no need to settle or accept anything less.

As you pursue the plan of action, working on the life list, other goals, and making the world a better place, these principles may help in the implementation:

**There is almost always more than one way to accomplish something.** If you begin your adult life on the conventional college track, you quickly learn the patterns and behaviors to which you are expected to conform. You're supposed to take a certain number of college courses each term; you need to select a major at some point; you're supposed to follow a fairly standard track that leads from History 101 to a graduation ceremony a few years later.

Then, you begin your first "real job." Your first job is supposed to be entry-level. At some point you move to a position in the middle, where most people spend most of their careers. Some move on to senior positions (partner, executive, tenured full professor), but this move usually comes after a long time in the middle. Granted, the specific expectations and job positions vary by industry—but almost all industries follow a similar pattern of apprentice, beginner, mid-level, and executive.

At every stage in this process, there is usually a fast track or alternative path you can pursue that will allow you to skip many of the steps that everyone else spends ages on. The alternative path (also called the "unconventional choice" throughout the book) is not only more efficient; it's also often more effective.

**When faced with a choice between abundance and scarcity, choose abundance.** Scarcity is the default mode of operation for most of us. It's a hard habit to break, but almost always worth it. Scarcity involves hoarding, and abundance involves sharing.

We'll look at this more in chapter 9, but in short, the choice for abundance typically involves a refusal to view the world as a zero-sum competition. No one else needs to lose for you to win (and vice versa).

**When faced with uncertainty about taking a leap of faith, take the leap.** You'll regret the things you didn't do much more than anything you did, so you might as well try new things. You also won't have to worry about burnout. When you do what you love, why would you burn out? (If you're going to worry about something, worry about regretting a decision you really wanted to make but held back from because of fear.)

**Intelligence is not a prerequisite, but determination is.** To take over the world, or do whatever you want to do, you don't need to be especially intelligent. In fact, in some cases high intelligence can be a handicap, because smart people are very good at making simple things complicated. You will, however, need to be fairly determined. This is because we live in a conventional world, and doing what you want can be surprisingly difficult. If you're afraid of sacrifice or lack the ability to stick with something you believe in, you might be tempted to give up along the way.

**You can have unlimited dreams and goals, but not unlimited priorities.** Almost every time I head out on an international trip, I end up talking with someone who expresses an interest in doing the same thing. Their statement is usually something like "Wow! I wish I could do that."

Here's the thing: I realize that there are plenty of people out there who are not able to travel or make the same choices I can. Having lived in the poorest countries in the world for four years, I know many of them personally. Most of the people I interact with now, however, as well as most of the readers of this book, don't fit into that category. The people I talk with now who tell me they "wish" they could do something but feel unable have usually made a number of choices that prevent them from doing what they wish. They have chosen to prioritize other things above their stated desire.

Some of them, I've noticed, can even seem a bit resentful of those who step out in a different direction. When I offered to help a friend plan an upcoming trip to Europe, she eagerly accepted. But then she said, "You know, not all of us can just take off and fly around the world like you do." I laughed it off and helped her anyway, but her offhand remark stayed with me after our conversation had ended. As I thought about it later, I realized that the statement reflected a common form of jealousy. This friend made more than $80,000 a year and certainly could have afforded to travel anywhere she wanted, but it wasn't her priority.

As you begin making more and more of your own choices, you'll encounter feedback like this fairly often. Many people are uncomfortable with change and different ideas, and they'll work hard at rationalizing their own choices when they come across someone who has made different ones. I'm not saying it's a bad thing for someone to prioritize a life around working at the office and buying things for their home; I'm just suggesting that they openly acknowledge that as the priority.

**If you get a few things in order, the stages of growth are exponential.** It takes many small businesses a long time to make $1,000 a month. I remember when I first made $1,000, I was ecstatic. Never mind the fact that I worked days and nights for several weeks to get the $1,000—when you're just getting started as an entrepreneur, it's sometimes better not to do the math.

> Sometimes the smallest decisions can change your life forever.
>
> —KERI RUSSELL

But to go from $1,000 a month to $5,000, it's not usually five times as hard. For some reason no one completely understands, it's usually only about twice as hard. In other words, if you can find a way to make $1,000 a month on your own, you can usually find a way to make $5,000.

The same is often true with personal habits. Have you ever known someone who changed a completely sedentary lifestyle to a completely active one? One year the guy is an overweight smoker who eats and drinks too much. The next year he undergoes a remarkable transformation where he quits smoking, radically improves his diet, and becomes a fitness freak.

We see those people and think, "That's amazing!" And on a personal level, it *is* amazing. But the most amazing parts are the first steps. Somewhere along the way, momentum kicks in and never stops. Momentum carries marathon runners from mile 24 to mile 26.2. It can help you scale up your life, but first you need to be very clear on what it is you want and where you are going.

## Your Life, Your Terms

Bernard Lopez, the cubicle dweller turned cross-country cyclist, described his moment of transition as an "indispensable decision." On one side was safety and routine, on the other side was uncertainty and adventure. A few days before leaving New York, a friend gave Bernard $50 to buy last-minute supplies. He went to the bike shop and bought a compass, something he had never used before but thought would be a good thing to have.

Later that afternoon, a moment of doubt set in as he realized he had no idea how to actually use the compass, or how it would actually be helpful when riding his bike. Laughing at how little he knew about the task ahead, he continued packing and set out anyway. Why not? He had gone too far to go back to his old way of living.

There are easier ways to live, but for many of us, they are far less fulfilling. Like Bernard with his bike journey, each of us faces an indispensable decision. Bo Bartlett, a professional artist who spent 20 years painting for free before his paintings started selling for $50,000 each, put it this way: "It is not the decision you make that is most important; it is the degree of commitment with which you make the decision."

If you're up for the commitment, victory is on your side in the long run. You *can* create the life you want, you *can* make the world a better place at the same time, and you *can* have it all. Just be prepared to work for it.

What matters most to you? How will you take over the world? Most important, what will be the terms of your unconventional, remarkable life?

### REMEMBER THIS

- The pathway to world domination, or whatever it is you want to do, begins with clearly understanding what you want to get out of life.

- Once you begin taking your ambitions seriously, you can usually accomplish most things in less time than you initially expect.

- In the end, it's not all about you. Most of us want a life that leaves a positive impact on others.

- When you start doing what you really want, not everyone will understand. This is okay.

# 3 Smashing Through the Brick Wall of Fear

*The absence of fear is not courage; the absence of fear is mental illness.*

—PO BRONSON

Sloane Berrent, originally "a geeky girl with big glasses" from Pittsburgh, stood at the top of a trash heap in the Philippines. Sloane had always been a traveler, having visited more than 40 states and 30 countries, but this was different. Here in Manila, she watched as professional trash scavengers picked their way through everything that had been discarded in the massive urban city.

Sloane had come to Manila as a Kiva fellow, with the intention to listen, observe, and help where she could.* Signing up for the four-month volunteer commitment was a big decision, and before she left Pittsburgh for the long trip to Asia, Sloane was simultaneously excited and nervous.

---

* Kiva is the leading organization that facilitates micro-lending around the world. To learn more about their great work, visit Kiva.org.

It helped that Sloane had a history of making brave and unconventional decisions. Before heading off to volunteer for Kiva, she had bootstrapped her way into an executive job at the age of 25, earned an MBA while working full-time, left Pittsburgh for a life in Los Angeles, and started her own charity. The question she gets asked most often—over and over from family, friends, and observers—is why isn't she afraid to try so many new things? As an outsider, wasn't it scary to come to Asia and work in the trash heaps of Manila?

Here's what Sloane says about fear:

> The greatest mistake you can make in life is to be continually fearing you will make one.
>
> —ELBERT HUBBARD

*I'm scared every day. I'm scared people won't think I'm doing this for the right reasons. I'm scared since I'm everywhere at once and nowhere all the time I won't have the opportunity to settle down and have a family. I'm frightened something will happen to a loved one while I'm too far off to reach them and I won't be there for someone who needs me.*

*But here's the thing. I've also realized that fear is normal. If I didn't get a little tug in my stomach before something big, it wouldn't be the right thing. Fear is energy mangled and a powerful motivator, so I just turn it into something positive. When you're scared your senses are heightened. I use my fear to hone my intuition. I'm alone a lot in countries and situations people at home wouldn't be comfortable in, but nothing bad happens to me. Why? Because I make smart decisions, but also because I*

*use my senses and I trust my fear to have its place when there is*
*something to truly be scared of.*

I like how Sloane puts it. I enjoy rooting for Lance Armstrong as he tears up the Pyrenees, reading about Dean Karnazes running a 200-mile relay race as an individual contestant,
and watching Michael Phelps break more and more swimming
records. But here's the thing: sometimes it's hard to relate to
those people. It's kind of like the story I heard from the flight
attendant who served Brad Pitt on a flight. Brad was traveling
with a personal assistant in the next row and two bodyguards
who sat on either side of him. The personal assistant did all the
talking, and had her own set of utensils to taste Brad's food
before it was served to him.

"He was so nice!" the flight attendant told me later. "He was
really just a regular guy." I liked the irony—Brad Pitt may be
nice, but most regular people I know don't travel with two bodyguards and a food taster in tow. To most of us, when people
acquire an entourage or start running 200-mile relay races on
their own, we struggle when trying to compare our lives with
theirs.

If there's such a thing as being truly fearless, I haven't found
it yet. When I heard Sloane's story, the first question I had was
"How did she go from Pittsburgh to the Philippines?" In other
words, how does someone overcome the fear we all have to do
something remarkably brave? In Sloane's case, it wasn't that she
was fearless; it was that she found a way to accept the fear and
work with it to do something that mattered more.

When you choose to defy convention, you'll run up against all kinds of people who are resentful of your decision to chart your own path. With preparation and courage, you can usually find a way to stand up to those people, and other times you can just do your own thing and ignore them.

Be forewarned, though: the toughest obstacles most of us have to overcome are the direct result of our own fears and insecurities. It's good to get a handle on these issues before you worry about anyone else. If you're the rare soul who isn't afraid of anything and already embraces personal change, you can safely skip this chapter and continue on ahead. Assuming you're like the rest of the planet, this information is for you.

## What Are We So Afraid Of?

Fear begins with an undefined worry, a voice in the back of your head that says you're not good enough, you won't succeed with anything big or significant, and you might as well give up and stop trying to stand out. The implied message is, "Who are *you*, anyway?"

We often imagine these words as coming from other people, perhaps someone who hurt us long ago or a negative person still involved in our life. These voices are not entirely irrelevant—the consequences of neglect and abuse are real—but it's also true they can be manufactured or exaggerated by our own insecurities. Because the biggest challenges we face are often internal, we need to deal with them first.

When we really get serious about our insecurities, we usually find that three specific fears emerge: the fear of failure, the fear of success, and the fear of change. The greatest of these is the fear of change itself. Whenever we take a big leap, we know that no matter what happens, our life will probably be different. To many of us, taking that leap is scary.

> Always do what you are afraid to do.
> —RALPH WALDO EMERSON

All things being equal, we generally resist change until the pain of making a switch becomes less than the pain of remaining in our current situation. This is why incompetent or even hostile employees are allowed to remain in a job far longer than they should, because managers don't want to deal with finding someone else to replace the bad apple. It's also why people accept all kinds of situations that are unproductive or downright harmful, from jobs that drain their energy without producing much in return to dysfunctional relationships. To break the cycle, the fear of the unknown has to become less than the stale acceptance of the current situation. There are two ways to make this happen:

- Increase the pain of the current situation

- Decrease the fear of the desired situation

Sometimes we don't get a choice in deciding between the two options. Let's look at an example I call a "watershed moment"— you'll see why in the story below.

## The Great Apartment Disaster of 2008

I love to travel, and I don't mind the stress and logistical hassles that some people are bothered by. You can throw flight delays, absurd security checks, or long bus rides at me and I'll keep smiling throughout most of it. When it comes to actually *moving* somewhere, though, I hate it. From start to finish, I don't like anything about the process. I feel guilty about owning too much stuff, I don't enjoy packing boxes, I worry about leaving things behind, and I worry about taking them with me. On moving day, I revert to the lowest evolutionary level of humanity: I can pick up boxes and stack them in the U-Haul, but that's about it.

One recent December, Jolie and I returned from a vacation to find our apartment flooded due to a broken pipe in another unit. The pipe had burst over the holidays, and no one had noticed for a while. While we had been away, an emergency repair crew had entered both units, dismantled our bed, and carried the pieces out to the living room—along with all of our clothes and everything else that had been in the room. The carpet in the bedroom and all the way down the hall was also removed, leaving the hard floor below and a generous helping of nails waiting to be stepped on.

At first I was annoyed, but I tried to operate under the principle that it was an accident and everyone involved in fixing up the unit was acting on good faith. We set up camp in the living room for what we thought would be a night or two. A night or two stretched into a week, then two weeks, then nearly an entire month. During that time we continued to sleep on a mattress in the living room, a situation we termed "urban camping" in an attempt to stay positive.

While camped out, I learned an important lesson: the greater the number of insurance companies that are involved in a construction project, the more likely it is that none of them will take responsibility. Each representative we talked to agreed that the damage was not our fault, but no one was willing to pay for us to stay elsewhere during the repairs.

As the weeks went by, I experienced a growing conflict between two undesirable alternatives. It wasn't fun to sleep in the living room and plan our lives around various work crews all day. Despite the discomfort of moving, after 10 days of little progress, I finally began to think about making a change. We had happily lived in the apartment for more than two years, but this situation was really pushing us to the limit.

Then I went away on an overnight trip, and Jolie called me at 11 p.m. to say that we had no water. After a few tense calls to the landlord and the construction supervisor, we still didn't know what was going on. The water might be coming back on in the morning, or it might be coming back in two weeks. Who knows? The implied message was that we should be grateful for our not-so-nice apartment and the mattress on the floor of the living room.

Hearing the news about the water sent me over the edge. I

could deal with urban camping and bogus insurance companies, but I wasn't willing to deal with not having water for an undetermined period of time. At that moment, the pain of remaining in the situation became greater than the pain of making a change. That was the moment I became ready to move. Jolie agreed, and we immediately started looking for a new home.

Less than three weeks later, we moved a few hours south of Seattle to a new home in Portland, Oregon. We hadn't really planned on changing states, but since both of our careers are flexible, we decided it would be about as much trouble to move to a new state as it would be to move across town. We had been interested in Portland for a while, and we took advantage of what was originally a negative experience in the form of a flooded apartment. I'm glad we made the change, but it never would have happened if the pain of the apartment situation had remained strictly an annoyance instead of the disaster it turned into.

## Overcoming Fear:
## The Twin Stories of Sean and Aaron

When the apartment was flooded, I was forced into thinking about change. In other situations, we have much more choice in the matter. Because I've been self-employed for most of my life, I often meet with people who want to know how they can take more control of their own lives by embracing entrepreneurship or another kind of unconventional career.

These meetings have been with people from diverse backgrounds, including students, engineers, journalists, artists, and investment managers—just to name a few. All of them were interested in creating an unconventional career. What they *differed* in was the level of awareness of their own "quiet desperation." Some were interested in self-employment merely as a possibility, whereas others would do anything they could to get closer to the goal. To put it another way, some of them were ready to embrace the uncertainty of change, and others weren't.

I'll tell you two stories to illustrate this important distinction. These stories are not composites (they are both completely true), but it's also fair to say that the patterns in each of them have been repeated time after time.

## STORY 1: SEAN

Typically, the people who are ready to change want the change more than almost anything. They want a way out of their current situation, and could we do it yesterday, please? One of the people I've met who fit this description is Sean Ogle. Just 23 years old, Sean had been working his first major job as a financial analyst for just over a year. Due to a combination of intelligence, diligence, and being in the right place at the right time, the job was a cut above the usual entry-level position most college grads receive.

Sean was making more money than most of his peers, and after starting work he made the first big purchase of his life: a 2005 Subaru Legacy GT. There was just one problem: he hated the job. Every day he sat in a small office, staring at the walls and wishing he was anywhere but there. With the remaining funds in his savings account, Sean took a trip to Brazil with a friend. That's when the big shift came. Brazil, and what it represented, was good. The desk job at home was bad. "Basically," he told me with a look of resolve during our first meeting, "I'm willing to do whatever it takes to get out of this situation."

We talked for a while and I gave him a long list of resources. "Will you have time to look at these things soon?" I asked.

"Are you kidding?" he replied. "I'll be going on this stuff for the rest of the afternoon. Then if I have to, I'll stay up until midnight."

On the way out of the coffee shop, we passed by his Subaru. "Nice car," I said.

"It's nice," Sean agreed. "But I'm going to sell it. This car will not take me where I want to go in life."

Sean sounded pretty serious, and I was almost convinced. The only thing that kept me from being fully persuaded was the reminder in the back of my head that I had heard this story before. We'll come back to Sean's story in a moment—but first, let me tell you about Aaron.

## STORY 2: AARON

When Jolie and I lived in West Africa, we returned to the United States once a year to visit family and friends. During that time, we would also speak at various events to raise money and awareness for the work we were doing overseas. After the last talk during our first year back, a guy approached me in the back of the room. He was interested in volunteering and wanted to talk with me later that evening.

To be honest, I didn't want to continue the conversation that night. We were getting ready to fly to Amsterdam the next morning, we needed to say goodbye to our families, and we still hadn't packed. Aaron* was desperate, though—in a good way. It sounded like he was pretty serious, so I looked at Jolie, she nodded, and we said yes.

At 10:30 that night, Aaron came over and we talked for an hour while Jolie and I packed our bags. We told him all about Africa, what our organization was doing, and how he could help. Aaron was eager and asked lots of good questions. After an hour, we really had to finish getting ready to leave in the morning. I kept looking at my watch, and he finally got the hint. We said goodbye, and Aaron said he would be in touch.

Jolie and I flew to Europe and met up with our friends before continuing on to West Africa. In the hustle of the work, I forgot about Aaron, and he never got in touch. One year later, we visited the United States again and spoke at another event. Guess what? Aaron was sitting in the front row. He came up to me afterward looking a little sheepish. He said he had intended to follow up, but a number of other things had happened. He began a new relationship that he thought would lead to something serious, for example, and so he put the plans on hold.

But, he said, the relationship had ended, he was ready to

---

* Some details, including the name, have been changed in Aaron's story.

make a new start, and wanted to meet again with more questions. I met with Aaron in a coffee shop this time and we talked for 45 minutes. Many of the questions he asked were the same ones from the year before. My answers hadn't really changed: here's the brochure, this is who you talk to, this is what you need to know, you just need to get started. Aaron kept saying, "I really want to do this," but always with a trace of hesitation. When we said goodbye, he promised to follow up again.

Another year went by, and I never heard from Aaron. We flew home from Africa again, and one day at the same coffee shop, I ran into Aaron for the third time. We had virtually the same conversation we had already fully explored twice, although this time my answers were a bit shorter. The whole time I was thinking, "What is it with this guy? He wants this so bad, but he isn't willing to do anything to get it." I ran into Aaron one final time the last year we were back, and I wasn't surprised to hear he was doing the same thing he was when we first met.

Perhaps Aaron just wasn't ready, and his time will still come. But every year as I saw him in that coffee shop, I always felt sad for him. I felt like Aaron wanted someone to take him by the hand and make decisions for him—something that wasn't likely to happen.

Meanwhile, Sean didn't wait for the opportunity to come to him. Sean followed Andy Warhol's advice, "They say time changes things, but actually you have to change them yourself."

I met with him again a month after our first meeting. He had a legal pad full of notes, tasks, and questions. I asked how things were going at work, and he smiled while telling me, "The good news is that I'm even more miserable than before." Things were so tense at the office that he had to tell his boss he was going to a doctor's appointment in order to meet me at the coffee shop that afternoon. On the bright side, he now spent several hours a day working on a new blog about his upcoming travel plans.

Being miserable in the day job had motivated Sean to get serious about doing something different. Over the next six months, he kept plugging along, paying off his debt and planning for a new life. He connected with a group of people building websites from Southeast Asia. He structured his life in a way that allowed him the freedom he craved. He sold the car. It wasn't always easy, but Sean made it work.

On September 15, Sean met with his boss to say that his "release date," as he put it, was drawing near. Sean offered to continue working for the company, but only if he could do it from on location somewhere far away from Portland. "Being willing to walk away from a job that most people thought was great felt scary and exciting at the same time," he told me. Two weeks later, his boss came back with an answer: thanks, but no thanks. Sean kept his part of the deal; he packed his bags, including the laptop he would use to create his own small business, and headed out for a new adventure in Bangkok, Thailand.

## Building Your Own Net

Bestselling author Paulo Coelho famously wrote, "When you want something, all the universe conspires in helping you to achieve it." Similarly, you may have heard the old saying "Leap and the net will appear." The skeptic in us may be quick to dismiss these ideas as self-help fantasies. I think there's actually a lot of truth to them, but even if you're not convinced, that's okay—we can reduce the fear and increase the odds of success before taking the leap. To do that, we'll build our own net and then take the leap. The process involves three steps: staring down the brick wall of fear, building the net, and smashing through the wall.

### STEP 1: STARING DOWN THE WALL

Conquering fear begins with acknowledging fear. Because our fears and insecurities are often illogical, it helps to break them down to the most basic level. You can do this by making a list of all the things you're afraid of at any given time. For my example, see the list on the next page.

Remember that most remarkable people were not born competing in the Tour de France or flying to Asia to climb onto trash heaps. Most of them were fairly average people like everyone else, who simply woke up from sleepwalking somewhere along the way. They made a few key decisions that forever altered the course of their lives—decisions like filling out an application or having a big talk with a boss.

## A FEW THINGS I'M CURRENTLY AFRAID OF*

- I'm only on chapter 3. Will I ever finish writing this book?
- What if it sucks? What if I get bad reviews? (Or worse, what if no one pays any attention?)
- I'm afraid of the forces of mediocrity and lethargy. I'm afraid of becoming too comfortable or getting lazy.
- When I travel, I'm afraid of trying to speak another language.
- Sometimes I feel paralyzed. People say they want to travel with me, and I think, "Oh no—then they would figure out that it's not always that exciting."
- I'm afraid that people will think I'm faking it.
- I'm scared of getting older and missing out on something I should have already done. (In the words of John Mayer, "I'm only good at being young.")

---

* Highly abbreviated.

## STEP 2: BUILDING THE NET

**Apply the "no regrets" mind-set.** After acknowledging fear, you then need to change your mind-set and prepare for making a change. A few years ago, while I was living in South Africa, I began to think seriously about living a life without regrets. I realized that even though I had been fortunate to have had a lot of great experiences at a young age, there were still a few areas of my life that were undeveloped. Among other things, I worried

a great deal about what other people thought of me, and I was
so afraid of disappointing them that I would allow that fear to
influence many of my decisions.

A few friends told me they were going to climb Table Mountain later in the week, and they invited me to come along. At
first I said, "No, I have a lot of work to do," knowing that I had
a meeting to attend and the other people at the meeting would
wonder why I was absent. For the next couple of days, the decision nagged at me. I finally called my friends back and went
with them to climb the mountain.

I know this sounds like a small decision—giving up one
morning's work—but at the time it felt incredibly freeing. I've
thought back on it many times as
I've moved on to other stages of life.
There are times, for example, when
I've reconsidered my decision to try
to visit every country in the world.
I could still travel without such an
exhausting goal, but I know that
I'd always regret it if I didn't try to
go everywhere. By applying the "no
regrets" philosophy, I experience a big
shift in perspective. I can climb mountains on a workday. I can
go to countries that most Westerners only read about. Twenty
years from now, I know I'll be glad I did.

> Inaction breeds doubt
> and fear. Action
> breeds confidence and
> courage. If you want
> to conquer fear, do
> not sit home and think
> about it. Go out and
> get busy.
>
> —DALE CARNEGIE

**Take the worst case scenario.** Asking yourself, "What's the
absolute worst thing that could happen?" if something goes

wrong can be very empowering. It helps you put things in their proper perspective.

To take it further, you can also ask, "Will the world end if this does not go the way I expect?" Shockingly, I've found that the answer is usually "no." In Warsaw last year, I went for a long run along the river, followed by a big breakfast at my hotel. Life was good. Then I logged on to check my upcoming travel plans. On what I thought was a routine task, I called Singapore Airlines to request a seat assignment for my flight back home from Asia the following week.

"I'm sorry, sir," said the friendly agent on the other line, "But I don't see your name on the manifest for that flight." This happens to me a lot—at any given time I have a series of complicated itineraries in progress, so I asked her to wait a moment while I looked up the record locator for this one. When I retrieved the printout from the bottom of my bag and looked at it closely, I did a double take. "Uh, I'll have to call you back," I said to the agent, and hung up the phone. To my dismay, I discovered that I had double-booked myself on two nonrefundable tickets from Tokyo to Seattle the following month. Due to my error, I had no way to get back from my current trip—which would take me to Asia in a few days, and then on home a few days after that.

At first, I panicked. There I was in Poland, scheduled to fly to Asia in a few days, and I had no way home a few days later. When I managed to calm down, I asked myself the "worst case" question: what's the worst thing that could happen? In this case, I'd be stuck in Japan without a way home, and I'd probably need to buy another plane ticket. It's not fun to buy a one-way ticket from Japan on less than a week's notice, but in the long arc of life, it's probably not that big a deal.

That's pretty much what ended up happening. I felt dumb for making the big mistake, and I didn't enjoy paying the credit card bill for the extra ticket—but the world didn't end. Whenever people ask me if things ever go wrong with my trip planning, I now have an easy answer: "Well, this one time in Warsaw . . ."

**Create mass accountability.** You can also create mass accountability to help you smash through the wall. Sean Macias (a different guy than the other Sean), struggled with quitting smoking for years. He finally got serious and set up a Twitter account called *rebootself.* The goal was to "reboot" everything about his life he was unsatisfied with, starting with quitting smoking.

Sean invited anyone who was interested to follow along with his goal. Each day he posted updates: "It's been 72 hours since my last cigarette . . . ," "One week down . . . ," "90 days without a smoke . . . ," and so on. More than a year later, he's now officially a former smoker and has moved on to other health-related goals.

**Give yourself a carrot.** Some people may be uncomfortable with linking rewards or punishment to achievement ("Shouldn't the process be enough?"). My philosophy is, hey, use whatever works. I bought a new round-the-world plane ticket when I sold the proposal for this book. Nine months later when I turned in the manuscript, I booked a trip to Armenia and Azerbaijan. Your carrots may not include trips to remote parts of the world, so naturally you'll want to pick something more appropriate for yourself.

## STEP 3: SMASHING THROUGH THE WALL

After we've acknowledged fear and prepared for the task ahead, we often come to a sticking point: what to do? Assuming you know what you want and are just having trouble seeing it through, one thing that helps is to force the active decision. This is where you stop wavering and decide one way or the other if you're going to take the leap.

Forcing the active decision is good for a couple of reasons. First, it often encourages us to step out in our fear, since we may realize that fear is the only thing holding us back. Second, even if we decide against the action we were considering, taking the active decision *not* to do it will at least get it off our mind. (Just note that when you let something go, you have to really let it go. Otherwise, you're no better off than you were before you forced the decision.)

Let's get back to the original story of Sloane Berrent, and the twin stories of Sean and Aaron. For her part, Sloane was able to conquer her fears and go to the Philippines, while lots of other people considered the idea but then dropped it. By acknowledging her fear and deciding to go anyway, Sloane arrived in Manila and launched into a new challenge that would help the people she served through Kiva while also preparing her for the next adventure.

On the other hand, despite a stated desire for change and the

## 16 MONTHS OF PREPARING FOR OPRAH

After my website was fairly successful, I wanted to branch out into doing video updates recorded on location from around the world. Even though my primary communication skill is writing, I knew that the Internet was shifting to more and more video content, and it's always good to deliver information in different learning styles.

There was just one problem: I was terrible at live video. When I first starting talking to a camera, I froze up. I had trouble maintaining eye contact with the camera, I rambled in my storytelling, and I used too many filler words like "uh" and "you know." As I watched the videos, the problems were obvious to me, but I also knew it would take a fair amount of practice to get better.

What to do? My writing was popular enough that it was being read by tens of thousands of people a day, and I had achieved a platform where my readers expected good things. I started making the updates anyway, usually doing several takes of each short clip and posting up the better ones. When I watched the first couple of videos, my verdict was "not bad." In other words, they weren't terrible, but I also knew that Oprah's producer probably wouldn't be calling for a while either.

As I suspected, most people were understanding, but I also received a few notes from honest readers: "Hey Chris, your presentation needs some work." They were right and I knew it, but I made myself keep going. Slowly, I got better. I took a major trip over the summer and made 12 videos on four continents. On a long flight from Miami to Los Angeles, I sat next to an actress who gave me some good advice. She said, "People don't want you to be an actor. They want you to be yourself."

I don't think there's any danger of my becoming an actor. But I overcame the fear, and slowly got used to the idea of talking to a small blinking dot on the top of my laptop. A rep from CNN wrote and asked if they could use some of the videos. Someone from NBC called and asked if I'd take one of their flip cameras and shoot footage of my world adventures. "Sure, I'll take your free camera and go on TV for millions of people." I'm still waiting for Oprah, but when she calls, I think I'll be ready.*

---

* A note to Oprah's producers: feel free to give me a call at 503-852-1465. I'd love to come to Chicago for an afternoon.

ability to do basic research, Aaron remained stuck behind the wall of fear. He lived a life of quiet desperation, peeking through to the other side but failing to dismantle the bricks. Meanwhile, Sean wasn't that different from Aaron . . . at first. He had different goals but the same desire to escape what he knew was an unsatisfactory life path.

I don't think Sean is a better person than Aaron. They are both smart, ambitious guys who studied and worked hard. The difference was that Sean was able to conquer his fears and Aaron wasn't. For both Sean and Sloane, the process of fear-conquering was never easy, but it was definitely worth it.

Most of us are like some combination of Sloane, Sean, and Aaron. We have big dreams and ideas, but we also have big fears. The quest to overcome fear is lifelong, and almost no one is truly fearless. Instead of pretending it doesn't exist, you have to be willing to smash through the brick wall of fear. You won't be the first to do it, and what you find on the other side might surprise you.

What's waiting for you on the other side of the wall?

**REMEMBER THIS**

- Fear is normal! The goal is to conquer the fear, not to avoid it or pretend it doesn't exist.

- The pain of making a change must become less than the pain of staying in the current situation.

- Most remarkable people are not remarkable by nature. Instead, they made a few key choices along the way that helped them overcome their fears.

- Asking yourself "What's the worst thing that can happen?" helps to put big decisions in perspective.

# 4 How to Fight Authority and Win

Progress is a nice word, but change is its motivator.
And change has its enemies.

ROBERT F. KENNEDY

At the end of the winter quarter in 2008, University of Utah student Tim DeChristopher stumbled onto this question during his final exam for an economics class: "If oil and natural gas companies are the only ones who bid on land auctions, do you think the auctions are fair?"

As an environmental activist, Tim's answer was predictable: hell no, they're not fair. Other parties with an interest in the land—including anyone concerned about the environment— are effectively denied the ability to lay claim to the land due to the millions of dollars required to challenge the Shells and ExxonMobils of the world.

Activists tend to fall into a couple of groups. Most focus on letter-writing, marches, boycotts, and other peaceful means.

A few become anarchists, choosing to directly sabotage companies or events they believe are causing harm. Neither group, Tim had observed, is highly effective. Anarchists get beaten up and thrown in jail, and no one pays attention to letter-writing campaigns.

> The question is not who is going to let me, it's who is going to stop me.
>
> —AYN RAND

Tim looked around for a third way. It just so happened that the week after he completed his final economics exam, a controversial land auction was taking place in Utah. Instead of merely expressing his anger on an exam question or waving a sign somewhere, Tim wanted to find a peaceful way to actually stop the auction from going forward.

On the day of the auction, Tim walked past a group of traditional protestors waving placards on the street, strolled into a Salt Lake City attorney's office, and was asked by a surprised clerk if he wanted to register as a bidder. He said yes ("Why not?") and was given a different kind of placard—the kind that you hold in the air to signify your intention to place a bid.

The bidding started, and Tim raised his placard high, beating every other bidder for the first plot of land. For the second auction, he did the same thing, and then again for every other auction that morning. By the end of the morning, Tim had accomplished several different things. First, his arm was sore from holding the placard in the air for two hours. Second, he was now the new owner of 13 plots of land, a total of 22,000 acres, for the rock-bottom price of only $1,700,000. As soon as he paid up, the auctioneer told him, the land was his.

Third, the company executives who had flown into Salt Lake on private jets were pissed off. When you bid against someone who doesn't have any money but insists on raising every bid you make, you have a problem. The executives marched out in protest, but not before their attorneys filed a complaint with the local police and the attorney general of Utah. As a college student who worked part-time, Tim wasn't walking around with an extra $1.7 million dollars in his pocket, so he was arrested for disrupting the auction—charges that were billed as "civil disobedience."

Then things got really interesting. The auction had taken place in the interim period of 11 weeks between the Bush and Obama presidential administrations. Bush administration officials rightly suspected that the Obama administration would reverse their decision to put the land up for sale. The hasty auction in the interim period was designed to create an irreversible sale of the land prior to a change in political power. By disrupting the auction, Tim successfully deferred the decision over what would happen with the land into the new administration—exactly the result he had hoped for.

> A critic is a man who knows the way but can't drive a car.
>
> —KENNETH TYNAN

When January rolled around and the new administration took over, the Bureau of Land Management rescinded the decision to auction the land and declared the results of the sale invalid. Twenty-two thousand acres of land were now protected by a federal mandate that could not be easily undone. There was just one remaining problem for Tim: the attorney general of Utah wasn't happy. Filing two felony charges against him, the state wanted to send a lesson to anyone hoping to follow Tim's lead and start bidding on auctions with money they didn't have.

> People will always try to stop you from doing the right thing if it is unconventional.
>
> —WARREN BUFFETT

Tim has vowed to fight the charges and is mounting an active defense, but he also says he's willing to go to jail. "If that's what it takes, I'll do it," he told me before an upcoming proceeding. "The efforts to sell the land illegally were worth stopping. I have no regrets."*

Nearly all people who choose unconventional careers or lifestyles, or who otherwise wish to challenge conventional beliefs, will encounter opposition from authority and the status quo. Whether you want to become an activist or just live life your own way, this chapter will educate you on the tactics that are used against non-conformists from all walks of life.

You'll also learn how to fight back through a combination of direct and indirect methods. Direct confrontation is best illustrated in the words of Keith Richards: "If you're going to

---

* For the latest updates on Tim's legal case, visit Bidder70.org.

kick authority in the teeth, you might as well use two feet." In fact, you'd *better* use two feet, because when you start attacking authority head-on, authority tends to fight back.

Thankfully, lashing out with a teeth-smashing kick is not the only way to fight. You can also fight indirectly by going around the obstacles you encounter, or by changing the rules of the confrontation. To start, let's back up and look at some tactics that are frequently deployed to hinder people from making their own choices.

## Marginalization and the Department of No

Why do people do what other people expect them to instead of what they really want? There are a number of reasons: inertia, fear of change, and no one's ever told them they don't have to, for example. But here's one more: sometimes people fall in line because authority figures are very skilled at keeping them in their place. Many of these authority figures are "gatekeepers," which can be defined as follows:

*Gatekeeper.* n. 1. A person or group with a vested interest in limiting the choices of other people. 2. An obstacle that must be overcome to achieve unconventional success.

Gatekeepers are especially effective at telling you which choices you have, thus giving you the illusion of freedom while simultaneously blocking access to what really matters. It's like asking, "Would you like *a* or *b*?"—without letting you know that *c, d,* and *e* are also valid choices.

In the case of Tim DeChristopher, the Bureau of Land Management pretended the auctions were fair because they were open to "everyone." In reality, very few opportunities are open to everyone—in this case, the auctions were open to everyone with at least $1.7 million to spare, effectively limiting the process to big oil companies.

Understanding that few opportunities are truly democratic is the first step toward successfully challenging authority. Generally speaking, universities are open to everyone who has mastered the skill of taking standardized tests. Churches and religious institutions are open to all who agree to adopt a particular doctrine that defines acceptable and unacceptable beliefs. If a member sways too far from the agreed-upon boundaries, that member will be defined as deviant and will be ostracized by the rest of the group.

You may not have to compete against Shell and ExxonMobil in a government land auction, but chances are you'll come up against your share of gatekeepers. When you apply for admission to college or for employment with a company, for example, you'll encounter gatekeepers who intend to determine many important aspects of your relationship to others in the institution. Among other things, they'll determine:

- Whether you're even worthy of consideration in the first place

- Whether the institution views you as a threat that should be guarded against

- How you stack up compared to others who are also interested in the institution (peers, other applicants, and the people reviewing your file)

- How much you should be rewarded (salary, scholarship, etc.) for your contribution to the institution

Gatekeepers are "no" people. They are skilled at swatting down ideas and coming up with all kinds of reasons why a request should be denied or why a particular strategy won't work. Many organizations have an entire Department of No, which usually goes by a disguised title such as Legal or Human Resources.*

The table below lists a few conventional ideas about institutions and compares them to an alternative interpretation that views them as gatekeepers.

## A Second Look at Conventional Assumptions

| CONVENTIONAL ASSUMPTION | ALTERNATIVE INTERPRETATION |
|---|---|
| Higher education trains students for a profession | Higher education reinforces social obedience and pressure to conform |

---

* I'm grateful to Seth Godin's Alternative MBA students for the "Department of No" title.

| CONVENTIONAL ASSUMPTION | ALTERNATIVE INTERPRETATION |
| --- | --- |
| Associations and organizations exist to protect people from harm | Associations and organizations exist to restrict our choices and enforce monopolies |
| Religious institutions provide answers and shared experiences to members | Religious institutions subdue members toward a common belief to increase their own power |
| Charities exist to help people | Charities exist to sustain themselves |
| Entertainment and publishing firms ensure a meritocracy in literature, the arts, and filmmaking | Entertainment and publishing firms establish a cartel that promotes mediocrity and hinders independent artists |

In the practice of each of the conventional assumptions, the status quo is maintained, order is enforced, and deviants are punished. Alternative ideas threaten the core and are excluded.

Note that the role of most of these institutions can be turned around to produce positive change as well. Only about 80 percent of my experience in higher education was a waste of time; the other 20 percent was important and useful. Religious institutions can facilitate communities of individuals and groups seeking to understand faith, where open-mindedness is welcomed instead of shunned. Charities can help people and then get out of business as quickly as possible, setting a good example through a great success story. Unfortunately, the exceptions are rare, and conventional authority will usually need to be challenged before the exceptions can flourish.

## FOOLING SOME OF THE PEOPLE, SOME OF THE TIME

Let's say you're a bad person who wants to get a bigger slice of the pie for yourself by taking it away from others. (I know you'd never do that, but just play along for a moment.) Once you understand just how much control gatekeepers can have, here are some of the tools you'd use to convince people to go along with your plan when you find your authority being undermined or challenged:

## THE "JUST BECAUSE" RESPONSE

Gatekeepers maintain their hold on power by convincing people that their roles are necessary. Why do we do things this way? "Just because." "Because that's the way we've always done it." "Because someone said so." When someone threatens tradition or asks questions, gatekeepers will appeal to a logic based on history, even if their recollection of history is incorrect.

## THE "FOR THE GOOD OF THE PEOPLE" RESPONSE

Closely related to the "Just because" response, this defense hinges on the belief that when someone goes astray or makes an unconventional choice, other people must somehow be harmed by that choice. It's like the case of the monkeys in the cage we looked at in the first chapter: if one monkey is allowed to eat the bananas at the top of the cage, then everyone will want some. We can't have a world where everyone eats bananas! Imagine the terror that would strike society. (Meanwhile, some of the people who limit other people's choices are eating plenty of bananas; they just want to keep the produce section closed to outsiders.)

## THE APPEAL TO A HIGHER POWER, OFTEN UNSPECIFIED

The higher power can be God, the boss, the system, the corporation, or the general powers-that-be. In fact, it is often deliberately vague—a reference to norms or informal rules of society, for example. People refer to the higher power when they aren't really sure why something is being done in a certain way, but they know that a "just because" answer won't suffice on its own. The answer is "Well, so-and-so said it, so it must be true."

## THE "THINGS WILL BE DIFFERENT WHEN . . ." PREDICTION

The words that come after "Things will be different when . . ." vary depending on the setting. Common words include "older," "children," and "responsibility." When I was young, I heard that things would be different when I was responsible for myself. Before I was married I heard that things would be different with two of us. Now one of the most common statements I hear in this category is "when you have children"—usually in the context of "You won't be able to travel the way you do when you have kids."

Perhaps that's true. Since I don't have kids, it's hard to respond—which is why this kind of straw man argument can be so effective for gatekeepers. On the other hand, I know a lot of people with kids who travel even more than I do. Vince and

Jeanne Dee have been on the road for three years and counting, living on $24,000 a year and taking their five-year-old to more than 30 countries. In some of the poorest countries in the world, missionaries and aid workers raise their children, providing them with a worldview and set of experiences that would never be possible at home. In other words, while I don't have children of my own, it seems it's indeed possible to travel or live another kind of unconventional life as a family.*

Because we encounter these tactics so often, we tend to accept them at face value. It's also difficult when the tactics are deployed forcefully, and you feel like you're alone in questioning them. As we saw in chapter 3, change can only come about when the pain of transition becomes less than the pain of accepting the status quo. When you're ready to embrace change and challenge the authority of gatekeepers, here's what you do.

## DEPLOY THE UNDERDOG STRATEGY
## (CHANGE THE WAY THE GAME IS PLAYED)

When Tim DeChristopher challenged the rights of the oil and gas companies to bid on public land, he found a way to change the rules of the game. Tim wasn't the first to complain about the unfairness of the auction, but he was the first to get creative and upset the balance.

---

* To follow the adventures of Vince and Jeanne Dee, visit SoulTravelers3.com.

Through an analysis published in the *New Yorker* that ranged from basketball to every war that has been fought in the past 200 years, Malcolm Gladwell showed how underdogs—sports teams that were widely expected to lose, armies with only a tenth of the size of the larger one, and so on—can turn the tables on the "Goliaths" they are matched up against. To begin, the article showed the odds for various "David vs. Goliath" match-ups in military battles over the past two centuries. In this case, we'll substitute "underdog" for "David" and "authority" for "Goliath."

### Results of Conventional Warfare

Authority kicks underdog's ass, as expected: 71.5%

Underdog defeats authority in an upset victory: 28.5%

We all like to root for the underdog, but if we had to put money on it, most of us would bet on the authority to win. As Gladwell's analysis shows, 7 times out of 10, Goliath will march straight to victory when traditional strategies are deployed. Interestingly, when the rules of engagement are switched and the underdog gets creative, the results are nearly flipped upside down:

### Results of Unconventional Warfare

Authority kicks underdog's ass, as expected: 36.5%

Underdog defeats authority: 63.6%

Even in a conventional war, Gladwell argues, underdogs can win 28 percent of the time. In a typical underdog battle, David may just get lucky and come out ahead when authority lets down its guard. But when the underdog adopts an unconventional strategy and changes the rules of the game, the percentage of victory jumps even further, to 63 percent. In other words, when the underdog deploys an unconventional strategy, the underdog is actually *favored* to win.* Despite all appearances to the contrary, if you were a smart bookie, you'd set your odds in favor of the weaker opponent.

What is the difference between the two situations? The difference is that in one situation the underdog *deliberately changes the rules* of the confrontation. Remember that gatekeepers are all about limiting choices (you can have *a* or *b*, but not *c* or *d*). The underdog strategy looks for alternatives. In Gladwell's article, the alternatives included Lawrence of Arabia choosing to take a roundabout 600-mile journey through the desert to surprise his enemy, the Biblical David declining to wear armor into the battle with Goliath, and an undermatched basketball team using a full-court press to confuse their opponent. Tim DeChristopher's alternative was to find a third protest option as an alternative to the unattractive options of letter-writing or violence.

In other encounters with authority, you can simply nod your head, smile, and then go out and do what you intended. As mentioned, it's easier to ask for forgiveness than permission, but thankfully, you don't really need to ask for either one very often.

---

* The full article from Gladwell is called "How David Beats Goliath" and was published in the *New Yorker* on May 11, 2009.

## MORALITY AND THE LAW

Martin Luther King Jr. famously noted that "nothing Hitler did was illegal in Germany" at the time. Slavery in the United States (and other countries) was not only legal for hundreds of years, but it was actually against the law to help slaves gain their freedom. Same-sex couples still lack the right to marry in many U.S. states and in the vast majority of countries around the world.

I'm not an anarchist; I'm a tax-paying, law-abiding citizen and don't have any desire to bring down the government. It's also clear, however, that there are times when morality and the law are on opposite sides. On those clear occasions where the law conflicts with morality, I support the side of morality through creative acts of protest—like what Tim DeChristopher did in Utah, for example.

Authority figures don't know it all. You know that, and I know that—but many of them devote a great deal of their time to convincing us that they are the experts who must be listened to. Chances are, a series of gatekeepers and other authority figures lie in the way between where you are now and where you'd like to go.

Resisting authority is largely an active process. If you threaten authority, be prepared for a fight. You can try to kick authority in the teeth like Keith Richards said, but if so, you'd better use two feet. Alternatively, you can get creative and find a way to change the rules of the game, like Tim DeChristopher did. Use stones and a sling instead of a sword. Go around the obstacles.

Either way, keep the words of an old Chinese proverb in mind: the person who says something is impossible should not interrupt the person who is doing it. Gatekeepers are good at interrupting, so you'll need to become good at doing the impossible.

**REMEMBER THIS**

- If you're not happy with the way something is done, you don't have to accept it.

- Gatekeepers are authority figures who seek to limit the choices of others—you can do *a* or *b*, but not *c*, *d*, or *e*.

- Gatekeepers are good at justifying their actions through circular reasoning. A typical argument involves the phrase "Everyone else is doing this, so why shouldn't you?"

- When challenging authority, direct confrontation is not always the best way. Instead, use the underdog strategy to change the rules of the game.

# INTERLUDE

## ALL THE THINGS YOU DON'T NEED

When you brush up against the internal obstacles of fear and insecurity and the external obstacles of gatekeepers and critics, it's easy to be intimidated into giving up. Thankfully, a lot of things we sometimes think of as prerequisites for success are actually quite unnecessary.

We've already looked at forgiveness and permission—how it's easier to ask forgiveness, and you don't really need anyone's permission for much of anything. It doesn't stop there. Here are some more things that are completely unnecessary for your success.

**You don't need experience.** Experience can sometimes get you in the door, but what really matters is where you are now and where you're going next. The past belongs on a resumé.

**You don't need years of preparation.** Well, technically you do need preparation—but you already have it. It's called life. Whatever has led you to where you are today is good enough to launch you into where you need to go next.

**You don't need paperwork.** Paperwork includes degrees, certificates, endorsements, licenses, recommendations, referrals, and so on.

**You don't need a mentor.** No one else will ever be as invested in your development as you. You can't outsource the responsibility for planning the course of your life.

Please note: It's not that these things are *unhelpful*. It's that they are *unnecessary*. You don't need them to do anything.

## WHAT YOU REALLY NEED

If you don't need most of those things, what *do* you need?

**You need passion.** You need to be absolutely passionate about what you believe in. If you don't feel passionate about anything, chances are you haven't discovered what you're really good at yet. Keep looking.

**You need a vision and a task.** The vision tells you where you are going; the task tells you what to do next to get there.

**You need the answers to the two most important questions in the universe.** What do you really want to get out of life? How can you help others in a way that no one else can? Once you have the answers, you'll be ahead of most everyone else.

**You need commitment to stay the course.** Many people give up too early. Can you continue in your quest for 10,000 hours or more? If so, you're on the right track.

Important: What's the big difference between the things you don't need and the things you do? Most of the things in the first category come from other people. All of the things in the second category are up to you.

Above all, you just need *enough*. You need enough money, enough time, enough courage, and so on. What is enough? It depends on the goal, and that's for you to decide.

But don't worry about what you don't have. When you let go of all the things you don't need, a lot of other things become much easier.

# PART II

# Reclaiming Work

It's tempting to believe that the secret to happiness is less work. Here's another idea: instead of giving up on the idea of work, why not find a way to make it better? The next four chapters will help.

# 5 Competence Is Your Security

Take your life in your own hands, and what happens?
A terrible thing: you have no one to blame.

— ERICA JONG

My morning routine is fairly typical: I pour myself a cup of coffee, go online, check my email, scan through a few blogs, then head over to the news. One morning during the height of the global economic crisis, in between articles on political polarization and celebrity watching, I noticed an interesting link from MSNBC.com: "100 Ways to Make Money in the Recession."

Great headline, right? Hey, it made me click, and I wasn't looking for a job or especially worried about paying the rent. I hopped over to MSNBC in curiosity, but as I skimmed through the list, I grew more and more confused. Almost every "way to make money in the recession" relied on working for someone else, usually through menial labor. Most of the suggestions had to do with part-time employment of various forms: delivering pizza, waiting tables, and so on. Less than 5 of the 100 ideas involved any kind of entrepreneurial project, and those were typically listed with cautionary warnings. ("You can also start an online business, but beware that most businesses fail. If you're not tolerant of risk, stick to a reliable paycheck.")

In other words, don't do anything to take responsibility for your own security. Better to work for the man at low wages and be thankful you aren't out on the street. This mind-set isn't unusual, but it's extremely limiting. Delivering pizza may pay for gas money, but if you want to create independence or earn more than just above the poverty line, you'll need to find a way to take matters into your own hands.

> If you limit your choices only to what seems possible or reasonable, you disconnect yourself from what you truly want, and all that is left is a compromise.
>
> —ROBERT FRITZ

If it seems like I'm picking on pizza delivery drivers, I don't mean to. Prior to my self-employment journey beginning at age 20, I spent a few months of my own driving around town with a stack of pies in the passenger seat. The real culprit here is the attitude behind the MSNBC article: when times are tough, you need the security of someone else's business to get you through.

I think a better statement is: when times are tough, you'd better get creative. A friend of mine likes to say, "I'm sorry you feel bad about not meeting your goals. What I would suggest is that you begin meeting your goals, in order to feel better." No one else can be responsible for your success or well-being but you. If you agree, what should you do?

This chapter is all about risk tolerance, and it's guided by the principle that taking control of your own career is *less* risky than trusting someone else to look after you. There's more than one way to guide your own career, and not everyone is well suited for self-employment—but when you look to yourself instead of anyone else for the answers, you're on the right track.

## Taking Responsibility by Taking Action

Of all of the things that are difficult to accept, this is definitely one of the most difficult of all. Here it is: your own competence is your best security. You can find your own way out of any recession or external event. This isn't about positive thinking, visualization, or anything "woo-woo." You don't have to put on a Native American headdress and pray for rain. Instead, you need to change the way you interpret events, and then take action to change your circumstances.

> Memorize and follow this never-fail recipe: get started. Don't quit.
>
> —BARBARA WINTER

There are a few ways to do this, but each involves the concepts we looked at in the first third of the book: setting the terms of your unconventional life, overcoming fear, and fighting convention by changing the rules of the game.

## OPTION 1: THE CASE FOR SELF-EMPLOYMENT

I don't necessarily think everyone *should* be an entrepreneur or small business owner; as we'll see in the next example, you can also become career independent while working for someone else. It's fair to say, though, that a significant group of us want to establish "full independence" by taking the leap to self-employment. For me and many others, self-employment (even if just in partial form) is the best way to cut the dependency cord.

I also think our perceptions about risk and entrepreneurship are colored by what we hear in the news. We're used to hearing about how many businesses fail without considering all the ones that succeed—or the fact that most entrepreneurs start more than one business over the course of a career.

> The gap between ignorance and knowledge is much less than the gap between knowledge and action.
>
> —ANONYMOUS

If you find yourself in that group, what kind of business should you start? Ideally, your project should be "location independent," meaning that you can operate it from anywhere in the world. This doesn't mean that you'll pick up and move to Kigali, but it's good to have the option of roaming around if you so choose. This also means that most microbusinesses are either based strictly on the Internet, or are primarily online with a small offline component. It's not the only way, but it certainly makes life and work a lot easier.

## THE $100 BUSINESS

Just as you don't need someone else's permission to live your own life, you also don't need a lot of money to start a small business. I've started five businesses in the past decade, and every one cost less than $1,000. In fact, before I spent the first $100, I had a very good idea whether each business would succeed or fail.

Granted, none of them have gone on to make me fabulously wealthy. But that wasn't the goal—the goal was to support myself so I wouldn't have to get a job, and by that measure, every one of the five businesses has been successful.

I'm not alone in this experience. I recently sent out word that I was looking for stories of $100 business startups that went on to long-term success and profitability. Here are just a few of several hundred that I learned about:

- The Denver TV news anchor who was laid off and started a "Yoga at Work" part-time business for the cost of a $9 domain registration. Within six months she was earning $2,000 a month.

- The brick installation company that started when the founder was laid off from a car dealership. He took $18 to Barnes & Noble to buy "some kind of business book," but ended up buying coffee and looking through books in the café. After a rocky start and a difficult partnership, the business brought in more than $150,000 in its third year.

- The "$50 and a bottle of oil" startup that grew to a $6 million business within five years.

- The "Retro Razor" project that launched from a Seattle bedroom after the founder ran out of Gillette blades on a trip to

Italy (cost: $75.87 for initial inventory). Retro Razor signed up for Amazon.com's partner program and sales went crazy.

More details are available in the "Online Resources" section of this book.

## Characteristics of Good and Bad Businesses

| GOOD | BAD |
| --- | --- |
| Creates assets that sell on their own | Trades time for money |
| Independent of the economic climate | Dependent on the economic climate |
| Location independent (can be operated from anywhere) | Fixed location |
| Flexible hours, so the owner can decide when to put in the time | Fixed hours, like a shop or service where customers drop-in |
| High profit margins and regular cash flow | Low profit margins and irregular cash flow |
| The business founder owns the intellectual property | Someone else (a franchise, usually) owns the intellectual property |

Note that a business doesn't necessarily need to have every "good" characteristic and no "bad" characteristic. The point is just that the more your project falls on the "good" side, the easier it will be to become successful and sustainable.

Having been self-employed for almost all of my adult life, I'm admittedly biased toward entrepreneurship. At this point, I can't really fathom the idea of working in a traditional job. I recently visited my bank to open a new account, and the process took 45 minutes. After the first 15 minutes of sitting there, I started getting antsy. I talked with the woman who helped me with the account, and I asked her, "Is this what you do all day? What happens when no one is sitting here and opening accounts?" She sighed and said, "Well, there's . . . research. And sometimes . . . administration. We used to be able to use the Internet during downtimes, but now we're not allowed."

Personally, I embrace freedom more than a regular paycheck, "job security," or any other benefit of traditional employment. I do realize, however, that not every job is as monotonous as that of a junior account manager at a bank, so it's fair to say that working for yourself isn't the only option. Let's look at a couple of others.

## OPTION 2: BECOME A ROCKSTAR
## AND REDEFINE THE TERMS OF YOUR JOB

Allan Bacon, a self-described "40-year-old average guy," had a great job. The job included a secure position, a good salary, a reliable bonus, and full benefits. There was just one problem: as great as the benefits were, the environment was driving him crazy.

"It was like I was diving without a snorkel. The harder I tried to move forward, the more stressed I got and the less I could breathe," Allan said. In an effort to find a snorkel, Allan started a series of what he called "Life Experiments"—small- to medium-size actions that would help him prepare for bigger changes. The "Life Experiments" included everything from visiting art museums on his lunch break to deliberately downsizing himsewlf to a lower-level job that he felt offered more opportunities.

Within a year, the lower-level job had expanded to more responsibility and a higher salary than the previous job. Emboldened by the success, Allan's next experiment led to a temporary move to Paris with his wife and three daughters. "I wanted my kids to see another place without just taking them on a whirlwind trip," he said. "Would we kill each other in a city apartment? Would we go crazy from having to navigate in a place where we didn't speak the language?"

Nobody killed anyone else in Paris, and Allan's confidence grew even more. Upon his return to the United States, he negotiated down to part-time employment with the company. That way he could still have benefits and a stable (albeit smaller) income while he started his own consulting on the side. One year later, he was no longer keeping regular hours at the office at all, although he continued to work part-time for the company. This change allowed him to receive the freedom he craved without sacrificing a relationship with a company he enjoyed—and it helped that he could continue to count on a reliable part-time income.

Allan traces the root cause of the transition to his "Life Experiments," even the simple things like visiting art museums or taking up photography on the weekends. In his words, the impact of the experiments was "way out of proportion" to the experiments themselves.

Over and over I hear from employees at stable companies like Google and Microsoft, who begin a long message by saying, "I feel guilty because my friends think I have it made, but I don't like what I'm doing." I don't think these people are ungrateful; if you don't enjoy the place where you spend most of your waking hours, I don't see how you have it made. Allan's story is a good example of someone who was able to reclaim his independence without completely going off on his own.

## OPTION 3: REDEFINE YOUR PLACE OF EMPLOYMENT BY HIRING A BOSS

Susan V. Lewis is a marketer and designer with the all-important superpower of getting things done. After a string of varied, fulfilling jobs (including sports reporter, program director, and painter), she had settled into a five-year stretch at an office where her colleagues didn't relate very well to her work.

Susan was frustrated and wanted to make a change, but she didn't want to join the thousands of other people who were looking for jobs using conventional methods. "More than 300 people apply for any job I might be interested in or qualified for," Susan said. "Proving on a single sheet of paper to a computer or disinterested HR specialist that I'm even qualified to begin with is a no-win proposition."

To avoid competing with hundreds of peers who all looked good on paper, Susan had to change the rules and make her own game. Instead of job-hunting, she decided to go "boss-hunting." She set up a website describing the project, where she posted her

CV and background, explained what kind of role she was look-ing for, and invited prospective bosses to apply.*

Susan believed that there wasn't much value in changing the rules halfway. Instead, she followed the process of hiring a boss to its natural end, interviewing multiple candidates and finally extending a formal offer with terms and conditions to the com-pany she liked the best. In addition to "boss applications" that came from her preferred city of Dallas, she also received applica-tions from companies in Boston, San Francisco, Toronto, Nash-ville, Austin, Chicago, and New York.

Ironically (or not), the best application she received came from a company that hadn't even intended to hire a new employee at that time. They had the idea for a new marketing person in the back of their heads, but until they heard about Susan's boss-hiring project, they hadn't actually planned to fill the position for a while.

Susan is a hard worker, but her success was not entirely related to her superhero power of getting things done. When 300 people apply for a single position, you have to find a way to stand out from the other rockstars. Much of Susan's success came from turning the job-hunting process on its head and doing something completely different.

I understand the objections to using Susan as an example: not everyone can make a website promoting their awesomeness, the concept has already been done, "that would never work in my field," and so on. The fact is, however, that when Susan started

---

* Read more of Susan's story at SusanHiresaBoss.com.

the project, people said it wouldn't work for her either. She dared to be different, and in doing so successfully changed the rules of the hiring game right at the lowest point in the economic crisis, when unemployment rates throughout the United States were hovering near 10 percent.

## Confessions of a Renegade Entrepreneur: My Story

For me, the options of redefining the rules of work were different from what they were for Allan or Susan. To be blunt, I wasn't qualified to do much of anything in the traditional workforce, and I wasn't good at the few part-time jobs I held before striking out on my own at the age of 20.

As described in chapter 1, I don't have a history of building multimillion-dollar businesses. What I do have is a history of survival through self-employment, by any means necessary. Over time I developed an appreciation of entrepreneurship as a force for good in the world—but in the beginning, I was mostly trying to pay the rent each month.

I've heard it said that an entrepreneur is someone who will work 24 hours a day for themselves to avoid working one hour a day for someone else. It's fair to say that was a good description of my work for a number of years. I didn't create any kind of sustainable infrastructure; I did everything myself. For better or worse, if I didn't feel like doing something, it just didn't get done.

I'd be the first to say that this isn't the smartest model to follow, and I'm not necessarily defending it. For my early years, though, it worked just fine for me. I was focused on other things—four years in Africa, playing music at night, traveling, graduate school, and so on. I wasn't getting rich, but I had all the money I needed to do most of what I wanted. Once I had earned enough for the month, I stopped worrying about it until the next month.

After moving overseas, I continued to support myself through moonlighting, consulting on Google Adwords accounts and building websites for clients in the United States and Europe. At first the work took only a few hours a week, but in my third year abroad, a new information publishing business I had started on a home visit began to take off at the same time my volunteer responsibilities were picking up. My colleagues and customers in the business, which was based in the United States, had no idea I was living in Africa, and my non-profit colleagues in Africa didn't know about my second life on the Internet. A couple of times a month I'd set my alarm clock to wake up for 3 a.m. conference calls by satellite phone, where other participants would marvel at working on location from Los Angeles and London. I never said a word about being even farther away, in places like Sierra Leone and Liberia.

I worked 45 hours a week on volunteer projects and at least 20 hours a week on the business. It was all going well—or at least, as well as could be expected, but one evening, the duct-taped operation fell apart. I had just returned from a long day in the field, delivering medical supplies to a village two hours away from the capital city where we were based. I went online through the flaky satellite connection and began downloading email. I thought I'd spend 20, maybe 30 minutes processing messages and uploading orders before calling it a night.

Then I read the message titled "Urgent Update" and saw that it was from my new fulfillment center. The message explained that they were shutting down the company, effective immediately. "No more orders will be shipped," the owner said, and in fact, no orders had been shipped in three weeks. When I frantically called in on the satellite phone to get more info, the number was disconnected.

In retrospect, I should have seen the distress signs—inventory not being added to the database, a halfhearted response to inquiries—but in between delivering truckloads of relief supplies and helping bring patients in from all over the region, I simply missed it. Reading that email on a faulty Internet connection late at night in my small office, I sat and wondered what in the world I could do. I had a huge crisis on my hands, not much time to deal with it, and I was doing important work in Sierra Leone that I couldn't just leave behind to fly back to the United States.

Within a few hours, other business owners left out in the cold chimed in on several online forums to fume at the company that had left us all without a crucial link in the supply chain. I was mad too, but I knew that concentrating on the anger wouldn't help me. The fulfillment center would still be out of business, and I'd still be stuck without a way out of the crisis. The better answer, I knew, would be to focus on a solution to the problem. I could deal with the negative feelings later.

I called back home to my brother, who had first helped with the business more than five years earlier but now had his own career. "Ken," I said, "I'm going to need your help." My plan was for him to sign up as my temporary, one-man fulfillment center while I worked on a long-term solution. Thankfully, he was up for the task. Next, I called my printer to order new supplies, three new fulfillment centers to see if they could help, and several other customers of the failed supplier, to check out the new options. Over the next ten days, we replaced $20,000 worth of product and found a new supplier willing to accommodate a number of "refugee clients" from the failed fulfillment center.

At first, the process of sorting out the mess was extremely stressful. During the first few hours, I had no idea if I could recover from such an unexpected problem. Sitting there after I had made my last phone call around midnight, however, I began to experience a deep sense of calm. As strange as it was, I felt that in some ways the crisis was even a welcome event. It forced me to reevaluate what I was doing and to think creatively about solving the problem without dropping too many balls.

"This will all be okay," I wrote in my journal while on hold with one of the vendors. "I'll find a way to get through this and be better for it in the end."

And in fact, it *was* okay. My brother did a great job as a one-man shipping agency for three weeks, the new fulfillment center took over after that (providing much better service than the first one ever had), and I gained a new sense of confidence that I could handle any problem that came my way.

The lesson I learned was that you can come back from

anything. Even if your supplier disappears off the map and you are 5,000 miles away, a creative entrepreneur has to be able to patch things together somehow. No one else can be bear the blame, or the responsibility for the comeback.

Paradoxically, when you manage to survive a crisis that had "deathblow potential," you'll often end up stronger than you were before the walls fell down. The best part of all was that most people around me had no idea what was going on. My faraway customers were happy, and my non-profit colleagues in Africa never knew about the crisis I was dealing with in the evenings. I continued the volunteer commitment for another year before relocating back to the United States for graduate school, and I even slowed down the extra hours I put in while the business continued to grow.

## A Cautionary Note on Your Escape Plan

Of course, the above scenario could have gone another way—my attempt to resurrect a business on the verge of cardiac arrest could have failed completely. Even if that had happened, however, I'd still have been better off than working in a bank and dreaming up escape plans. Speaking of that, "escape" is a common theme of many self-employment resources, and I can understand why. When you work in the bank where you can't use the Internet, escape is probably the foremost thing on your mind.

But be careful. When you focus on escaping the humdrum of the cubicle (or wherever you spend your workdays), you also need to have something to escape *to*. Otherwise you may end up no happier than you were prior to the escape. Like the bride and groom who spend dozens of hours planning a wedding but little time actively planning the life they'll share after the big day, the other side of escape may be abrupt and unfulfilling instead of the exciting adventure it should be.

I'm also skeptical of the idea of eliminating work or reducing it to its most limited elements. It's not that I think there's anything wrong with making more time for family or activities you enjoy. I just think that if someone is unhappy with how they are spending their workday, the answer is to find better work. Personally, I like work. I believe in a 168-hour workweek that is filled with activities I love. A few hours of sleep can be thrown in if necessary.

Whatever side of that issue you come down on, the most important thing is to take the control of your career into your own hands. Entrepreneur, rockstar employee, creative professional, or somewhere in between—the best job security is your own competence.

### REMEMBER THIS

- No one else will be responsible for you or care about your well-being as much as you.

- You can create your own security in a regular job or by working for yourself. (I think working for yourself is easier, but it's not the only way.)

- Like Allan Bacon's "Life Experiments," slow and steady change can produce big improvements when done consistently over time.

- Some people think self-employment is risky, but the real risk lies in deriving your security from an external source

- Don't just escape from something; escape to something

# 6 Graduate School vs. the Blogosphere

> Some people get an education without going to college; the rest get it after they get out.
>
> MARK TWAIN

Why do students go to college, university, or graduate school? Presumably, the answer is that they would like to advance their knowledge or meet entrance requirements in a career that requires more education than they currently have. For some fields and some students, no doubt, this makes sense. Other students pursue higher education just because it sounds like a nice thing to do. I should know: I was one of them.

My undergraduate career was relatively undistinguished, aside from two things. First, I skipped high school to go straight into college. I wasn't a genius or kid wonder—I was just bored with high school and not good at following rules. After one disastrous year and one decent year where I was awarded the prize for "Most Improved Student," I decided to consider the award as a diploma and just didn't go back for the third or fourth year.

Yes, I was a high-school dropout, although thankfully I didn't continue on the conventional dropout path. The same year I quit high school, I enrolled in a local community college. By the time the registrar's office noticed that I had never finished high school, I had already finished the first full quarter. My grades weren't perfect (one A and two B's), but they agreed to let me keep going. "This isn't Stanford, you know," one of the administrators told me.

> The dumbest people I know are those who know it all.
>
> —MALCOLM FORBES

A couple of quarters later, I had racked up enough credits to transfer to a four-year university. Like my community college, it was far from prestigious (a small state university with 3,000 students), but I enjoyed the fact that I was now a fully enrolled college student without a high school diploma.

My grades were all over the map—straight A's for the major I would eventually stick with (Sociology), and several C's and D's from the classes I simply gave up on. In a pattern that continues to this day, I worked harder than anyone I knew on the subjects that I liked . . . and for all the other work, well, the results weren't pretty.

The other distinguishing fact about my college experience was that after I settled in, I realized that it wasn't difficult to achieve good grades (at least in the subjects I cared about) without a lot of effort. Carefully studying the course catalog, I began registering for the maximum course load each quarter. The first quarter I did this, I also had to take another class back at the community college. That gave me an idea: I couldn't register for more classes at the university because I was already at the limit, but there was no rule against attending multiple institutions simultaneously.

In a flurry of registration, I signed up for more and more classes each quarter—at the university, at the community college, at a second community college, and by correspondence with another university a few hours away. Taking as many as 40 credit hours one term, I graduated with two bachelor's degrees right at the end of my second year. My friends from the brief time I had spent at high school were just completing their freshman year.

> Colleges are like old-age homes, except for the fact that more people die in colleges.
>
> —BOB DYLAN

I don't have any regrets about the college experience, but I also don't have any illusions that I learned much in the way of actual content from the courses. Instead, I learned how to bluff my way through exams, how to quickly memorize (and quickly forget), and how to make myself look good. These are important skills in college and life, no doubt, but they can also be a hindrance on creating anything of lasting value.

A few years later, as I was coming to the end of my time in West Africa, I wondered if I had missed out on something. In the volunteer role, I was an executive in the field of International

Development, but I had acquired the role without a lot of training. Planning to return to the United States the following year, I applied for a master of arts program in International Studies at the University of Washington. In my application essay, I noted that in Liberia there was no location where I could take the required admissions test. "We're working on disarmament first, then clean drinking water, then electricity, and after that we'll think about standardized testing," I wrote. I also noted that the University of Washington was the only school to which I was applying. Most graduate school applicants apply for several programs, so my theory was to make it clear that I was going "all-in" and would definitely come if I was accepted.

If it sounds like a gamble, perhaps it was—but I saw it as a calculated risk. I knew that if I actually took the test, I would score poorly on it compared to students with a more traditional education. I had essentially no higher math skills and had been out of undergraduate school for five years. My theory was that the lack of test results accompanied by a good story was better than mediocre test results accompanied by a traditional application. By some miracle, the gamble paid off and I was accepted— and awarded a "Top Scholar" $2,000 prize, which I thought was ironic but happily accepted.

Because I had raced through college a few years prior and then avoided the standardized tests, I thought I'd be behind most of my fellow students when it came time to start classes that fall. At first, this assumption was correct: my peers used jargon I had never heard before, entire classes were devoted to books I'd never read, and my initial attempts at essays were returned with below-average grades and lots of red ink.

After the first quarter, though, I figured a few things out. Once again, I registered for the maximum number of credits and started writing my thesis a year early. I finished two quarters later with a 3.8 GPA and the chance to continue toward a PhD, but at that point I was ready to move on. Instead of attending the graduation ceremony, I went to India for two weeks of independent travel. By the time I came back, my diploma had arrived in the mail.

## The Cost of Becoming an Expert

This story is not about my relative academic success.* The story is about the value of what I gained in graduate school versus what I started working toward at the same time: becoming an authority through online writing. If the goal of graduate school is to prepare students for a more advanced career, it's fair to measure that goal against alternative methods.

As usual, I was involved in a lot of activities during the first half of 2008. I ran a marathon, traveled to more than 10 countries, finished a commitment as a board member for a non-profit

---

* It really is relative, because I knew many students much more serious than I was about academic affairs. I don't mind admitting that I was more interested in distilling information and completing the program than in becoming a highly specialized expert.

organization, and had plenty of other fun experiences. The two most important projects I completed were:

- Finished my MA program at the University of Washington

- Officially started the Art of Non-Conformity (AONC) site and built it to a respectable level within the blogging community

While these projects were being completed, I was faced with a decision to either continue my education with the PhD program on the East Coast or stay in the Pacific Northwest and focus on writing. I chose the writing, and I'll show you why here.

It all started with the observation that my MA thesis was read by a grand total of three people. Each of them said nice things about it, but the audience was extremely limited. By contrast, an online manifesto I published around the same time was downloaded (and presumably read, or at least glanced at) by more than 100,000 people in the first six months of publication.

That experience made me realize that my online work had the potential to make a much more significant impact on the world than any graduate education I could pursue. I know that there will be some questions about this comparison, so stick with me and I'll try to answer them before we close out the chapter. For now, take a look at the following table. Academics like to break things down in a comparative perspective, so let's look at a few factors a bit closer.

## Graduate School vs. the Blogosphere

| | TRADITIONAL MEANS OF OBTAINING EXPER- TISE (GRADUATE SCHOOL) | ALTERNATIVE MEANS OF OBTAINING EXPER- TISE (ONLINE WRITING) |
|---|---|---|
| *Financial Cost* | $32,000 | $8.95/month for hosting (or $5,000 for all expenses over a year) |
| *Time spent writing seminal work* | 40-50 hours (thesis) | 30-40 hours (manifesto) |
| *# of Readers* | 3 | 100,000+ |
| *# of Peers at Same Level* | 631,000 in one year alone | Less than 3,000 (or 22 Members of LifeRemix) |
| *Recognition as expert* | Moderate and highly specialized | Widespread and broad |
| *Field of specialization* | Governance and Development in Africa | Life, Work, and Travel |
| *Time spent on unproductive tasks* | 70% | 10-20% |
| *Outcomes* | Nice piece of paper | Highly active readership, speaking offers, side business, book contract |
| *Feedback from readers* | "Good job" from three people | Thousands of positive comments from all over the world |

**Financial cost.** Over the course of five quarters, I paid roughly $32,000 to attend the University of Washington's Jackson School of International Studies. This figure does not include books ($300 a quarter until I learned how to use the inter-library loan system) and other expenses related to obtaining my degree (a new computer, hundreds of pages of printouts for essays and term papers, gallons of coffee, etc.). I ended up graduating one quarter early, thus saving what would have been another $4,000 in tuition for the final spring quarter. To be fair, I also received a "free" bus pass and gym membership in exchange for my $32,000, which were both used and appreciated.

For my website, I paid $8.95 a month for hosting and began with a free WordPress theme I downloaded. Two photographer friends helped me with a photo shoot around Seattle one morning—they were kind enough to let me pay only with lunch—and I spent the first three months writing initial content that would help me when things got busy later.

As the site grew more popular, I paid more money to upgrade the design and add some new services (video updates, newsletter, and so on). However, I made these investments only after I had achieved enough initial success with the project to have a good estimation of what the improvements would be worth. In total, I probably paid about $5,000 over the first year—a bit more than one quarter's tuition, and funds that were recouped very quickly.

**Time spent writing seminal work.** The time spent writing and revising the seminal works (a 60-page thesis for graduate school and a 29-page manifesto for my website) was roughly the same. I spent approximately ten hours more on the thesis due to some last-minute revisions requested by one advisor.

**Number of readers.** After 40-plus hours of work, my MA thesis was read by a grand total of three people. I had the opportunity to publish a revised version of the paper in an academic journal, but the readership would have been very small and specialized. By the time I finished graduate school, I was busy with my new website, so I never got around to submitting the paper for publication.

By comparison, in the first six months of publication, the online manifesto was downloaded more than 100,000 times, by readers from more than 120 countries. Two years later, it continues to be downloaded by at least 50 to 100 new people every day, whereas my thesis ("Post-Conflict Governance and Stability in Liberia") sits unopened somewhere on my old laptop.

**Feedback from readers.** At the end of my thesis presentation, I was told I passed with distinction. That was nice to hear, but I only heard it from three people, and I don't think they've thought much more about my paper since our big meeting that day. Even if it was superb (which would admittedly be a big stretch), it certainly wasn't very influential.

By contrast, I've received thousands of emails and site comments from readers who read the manifesto. Some of them have made radically different life choices as a result of reading it. I've heard from people who have quit their job, changed careers, started a charity, left abusive relationships, traveled the world, and taken all kinds of other extremely meaningful actions. I don't think that my work was the sole motivation for these actions, but the fact that it was a significant part of the motivation is good enough for me. This kind of feedback continues to be one of the main reasons I write.

**Number of peers.** Just as the number of readers is an important metric of influence, the number of peers is also a good way to see how you stand out in the world. Each year, approximately 631,000 students complete graduate programs in the United States alone. In total, approximately 9 percent of the U.S. population has a master's degree or higher—relatively distinctive, but hardly unusual.

It is more difficult to judge the number of peers for online careers. Granted, there are millions of bloggers, but the vast majority are writing casual, primarily personal content. The AONC site is currently in the Top 3,000 sites in the world as ranked by Technorati. This ranking system can be somewhat arbitrary, but I think it's fair to say that my influence is far greater as a writer than as the recipient of a graduate degree.

I also became a member of the LifeRemix network, a small group of personal development and productivity authors. Among others, the group includes popular sites by Gretchen Rubin (*Happiness Project*) and Leo Babauta (*Zen Habits*), which allows me to associate with some of the most widely recognized authors in my industry. Within the LifeRemix network, I have exactly 21 peers, nearly all of whom have become personal friends. Being in a group of 22, or even a group of 3,000, is a lot more influential than being in a group consisting of 9 percent of the U.S. population.

**Recognition as expert.** My graduate degree was in International Studies, with a focus on development in Africa and a side concentration in Public Affairs. These are important topics, but I'm hardly alone in those fields. To stand out requires additional years, if not decades, of further training and publishing of academic papers read by a small audience.

For the website, I chose to focus my writing on "Unconventional Strategies for Life, Work, and Travel." This has led to my being viewed as an expert on alternative ideas for each of these areas. People write in by the hundreds every day, asking me which frequent flyer program they should join, how to charge their Nintendo DS in Asia, how to start a microbusiness, and all kinds of other topics. I still adhere to the guru-free philosophy and believe that people can obtain any information they need for themselves, but I'm happy to help wherever I can.

**Time spent on unproductive tasks.** My experience in academia was that I had to focus on pleasing people far more than doing good work. As mentioned at the beginning of this book, about 80 percent of the tasks and projects I completed for my degree had no lasting value, and judging from all the other students I hear from every day, I don't think my experience was unusual.

The opposite holds true in my new career: roughly 80 percent of what I do has some kind of lasting value. I can't claim to have eliminated *all* inefficiency in my writing career. I do a lot of things the slow-and-manual way, and some of my processes could definitely be improved. However, I'm comforted by the fact that about 80 percent of what I do is directly related to my overall goals of living the way I want while simultaneously helping others. If I never get beyond 80 percent, I think I can live with that.

**Outcomes.** After five quarters at the University of Washington, I received a nice piece of paper in the mail. No career assistance was offered. By contrast, my online writing has opened the doors to an entirely new career. Air New Zealand flew me to the South Pacific to write about one of their destinations. I've written for CNN, *Business Week*, the *New York Times*, and other A-list publications.

This book you are reading now is another product of that initial success. I regularly receive invitations for new opportunities—trips, speaking engagements, magazine articles, and so on. On this level, it's hard to even make a comparison between the experience of graduate school versus creating an independent career. It won't be the case for everyone, but for me, I've clearly found the better choice.

## Alternative and Independent Learning

What about the question of learning—you know, what higher education is supposed to be all about? Personally, I value learning, but formal education and learning do not always go hand in hand. If your primary goal is to learn instead of to prepare for a career, you may be better off going it alone.

Yes, there are exceptions. If you want to become a professor and work toward innovation in the academy, then you probably need the graduate degree. If you want to become a medical doctor, I suppose it's good that you don't learn how to cut people open with a "For Dummies" book. But the exceptions are greatly outnumbered by the rule that it is often quicker, cheaper, and easier to become your own expert.

If you value learning but aren't a fan of debt or busywork, why not create a way to learn what you need on your own? The One-Year, Self-Directed, Alternative Graduate School Experience offers a customizable plan to fit the needs of almost any aspiring student.

By following the alternative graduate school program, you'll gain the rough equivalent of what tens of thousands of other students regularly spend tens of thousands of dollars on. In return, you'll have gained approximately the same amount of knowledge (if not more) that you'd receive in a general social science or humanities program.

Naturally, if your field of interest varies, the program can be suitably modified. If you love literature, read 100 books instead of 50. If you're interested in computer programming, learn more than just how to blog. Now that universities are listing course materials online, in some cases you can even go through the same courses that paying students do. Download the syllabi for the courses you're interested in and listen to podcasts by professors.*

---

* In some cases, the course materials may only be accessed by registered students. To get access, write a short post on CraigsList or Twitter asking for help from a sympathetic student.

## THE ONE-YEAR, SELF-DIRECTED, ALTERNATIVE GRADUATE SCHOOL EXPERIENCE

- Subscribe to the *Economist* and read every issue religiously. Cost: $97 + 60 minutes each week.

- Memorize the names of every country, world capital, and current president or prime minister in the world. Cost: $0 + 3–4 hours once.

- Buy a round-the-world plane ticket or use frequent flyer miles to travel to several major world regions, including somewhere in Africa and somewhere in Asia. Cost: variable, but plan on $4,000. (Check the "Online Resources" section for more information.)

- Read the basic texts of the major world religions: the Torah, the New Testament, the Koran, and the teachings of Buddha. Visit a church, a mosque, a synagogue, and a temple. Cost: materials can be obtained free online or in the mail (or for less than $50) + 20 hours.

- Subscribe to a language-learning podcast and listen to each 20-minute episode, five times a week, for the entire year. Attend a local language club once a week to practice. Cost: $0 + 87 hours.

- Loan money to an entrepreneur through Kiva.org and arrange to visit him or her while you're abroad on your big trip. Cost: likely $0 in the end, since 98% of loans are repaid.

- Acquire at least three new skills during your year. Suggestions: photography, skydiving, computer programming, martial arts. The key is not to become an expert in any of them, but to become functionally proficient. Cost: variable, but each skill is probably less than three credits of tuition would be at a university.

- Read at least 30 nonfiction books and 20 classic novels. Cost: approximately $750 (can be reduced or eliminated by using the library).

- Join a gym or health club to keep fit during your rigorous independent studies. (Most universities include access to their fitness centers with the purchase of $32,000 in tuition, so you'll need to pay for this on your own otherwise.) Cost: $25–$75 a month.

- Become comfortable with basic presentation and public speaking skills. Join your local Toastmasters club to get constructive, structured help that is beginner-friendly. Cost: $25 once + 2 hours a week for 10 weeks.

- Start a blog, create a basic posting schedule, and stick with it for the entire year. You can get a free blog at WordPress.org. One tip: don't try to write every day. Set a weekly or biweekly schedule for a while, and if you're still enjoying it after three months, pick up the pace. Cost: $0.

- Set your home page to http://en.wikipedia.org/wiki/Special: Randompage. Over the next year, every time you open your browser, you'll see a different, random Wikipedia page. Read it. Cost: $0.

- Learn to write by listening to the Grammar Girl podcast on iTunes and buying *Bird by Bird* by Anne Lamott. Cost: $0 for Grammar Girl, $14 for Anne Lamott.

- Instead of reading the entire Encyclopedia Britannica, read *The Know-It-All* by A. J. Jacobs, a good summary. Cost: $15

TOTAL COST: $10,000 or less

---

\* The total cost of the self-directed, alternative graduate school program does not include housing or food, but neither does the tuition for traditional school programs in the United States and Canada. Freedom and Independence, however, are included at no extra charge.

## Objections

As far as I can tell, the three primary objections to the alternative graduate school program, or the practice of independent learning in general are (a) you don't receive a piece of paper at the end, (b) no career assistance is included, and (c) by studying on your own, you avoid "the experience" of being in class and on campus with other students and faculty. I've done my best to answer the objections below.

**No piece of paper.** True, if you study on your own, you will not receive a nice piece of paper at the end as an external recognition of your achievement. If you are so motivated by a piece of paper on the wall or a couple of extra letters on your resumé that you are willing to spend a year or more of your life in exchange for them, you'll likely need a traditional institution. Otherwise, you can forgo the papers and keep the life.

**No career assistance.** I spent $32,000 for my master's degree, and virtually no career assistance was included. The lack of help didn't bother me because I'm self-employed, but some of my peers who expected more were disappointed. If you *do* choose to continue with higher education, be sure you understand exactly what kind of career assistance you'll receive near the end of your studies. Just because there is a career office doesn't mean they'll do more than steer you to an HR website or bring a few recruiters to campus.

**"The experience."** The final objection to independent learning is that without entering into a structured program with other students, you won't benefit from a collective experience of working together and learning from others. This concern, I think, has some merit. Despite the fact that most of the academic requirements I completed were designed merely to keep the system moving along, I enjoyed some of the work due to the simple fact that others were doing the same thing. I also liked meeting new people, bonding together over shared commitments, and occasionally learning from faculty.

Therefore, I think the more important questions to ask are "How much is the experience worth?" and "Can the experience be obtained in another way?" The first question is highly personal—each person's answer will be different—but for me, the experience was probably worth what I spent on it although I don't see the need to spend any more at this point. Despite the likelihood that my writing career will continue to be much more successful than a career based on my graduate degree would have been, I don't regret paying the $32,000.

Since then, however, I've had a wide array of fantastic experiences that cost far less. Despite being a natural introvert, I've connected with thousands of like-minded people all over the world. Most of these connections were initially made online, but when we'd meet in person, we'd usually pick up where we'd left off. From Bangkok to Minneapolis, I've met readers in at least 20 cities so far. When I go to New York, Los Angeles, Vancouver, or even any number of smaller cities, there's always a group of people I can hang out with.

In short, I've found a way to do work that I love while still enjoying a wide range of social relationships—and I also benefit by not paying $6,000 or more per semester for the experience. This leaves more money for things I value, a topic we'll explore more in chapters 8 and 10.

## It's Your Life

When you consider investing large amounts of time and money in something, you should think carefully about what you'll get out of it. Several of my friends from graduate school agree that their time in the ivory tower resulted in a poor return-on-investment when compared to the limited gains they received later. Others, of course, are perfectly happy and wouldn't have done anything differently. That's why any form of higher education or alternative, independent learning should be evaluated on your own terms.

### REMEMBER THIS

- Relate your education to what you actually want to do when you finish.

- Don't use graduate school, or any other course of study, as a form of life avoidance. Pursue the course only if there's a good reason.

- Much of higher education consists of learning to make yourself look good. It's an essential skill, but you might as well learn something else while you're there too.

- Regardless of how you feel about college or university, consider some form of alternative learning to increase your knowledge.

# 7 The Power of Your Own Small Army

I start with the premise that the function of leadership is to produce more leaders, not more followers.

—RALPH NADER

Let's return to the story that began in chapter 1. Like many others after the tragedy of 9/11, in the fall of 2001 I became depressed and introspective. I had been in lower Manhattan a few days before the towers fell, and the experience naturally led me to reflect on the value of life and what I was really contributing to the world.

At the time I was working part-time in the mornings on my own business and playing jazz music with local bands at night. I enjoyed both activities and had a lot of fun, but I kept thinking, "There must be more." One night I went online and read about the horrific civil war in Sierra Leone that had left the country completely devastated. Throughout the previous decade, a violent conflict between rebel fighters and government forces had caused tremendous damage to the country and its people.

Then I read about Dr. Gary Parker, a plastic surgeon originally from California who had given up a lucrative practice for
a volunteer opportunity in West Africa. Plenty of doctors fly
off to the ends of the earth for a short volunteer stint, but Gary
was different: he had been living in a small cabin on a hospital
ship for more than 17 years. Instead of doing face-lifts in Santa
Barbara, Gary spent his days recon-
structing faces that had been disfig-
ured by tumors and war wounds.

> If your actions inspire
> others to dream more,
> learn more, do more,
> and become more, you
> are a leader.
>
> —JOHN QUINCY
> ADAMS

Along the way, he met Susan,
another volunteer, who became his
wife. Gary and Susan had two children, and the Parkers lived as a family on board the ship. While I was
sleeping in every day before heading to Starbucks for my morning coffee, they were all stationed in Sierra Leone—the poorest
country in the world according to the U.N. Human Development Index.

As I read Gary's story, I thought to myself, "If a surgeon
could give up 17 years of practicing in California to work in
war-torn countries, the least I can do is go and see what it's all
about." I was intrigued by Gary's example of selflessness, and I
wanted to be a part of it. Some of the attraction was the idea of
helping others, but it went beyond altruistic motives. Walking
around in a daze after 9/11, I saw the opportunity to be a part of
something bigger than myself as a way out of my depression.

A few months later, Jolie and I left our comfortable lives in
the United States to move overseas. We went to Sierra Leone

and moved on board the same ship as Gary, Susan, and their children. All in all, we spent four years working with them in eight different African countries, and those years were far more influential to me than anything I had learned in college or my early work as an entrepreneur. Gary was a leader I was willing to follow, and I eagerly enlisted in his small army of volunteers.

## Why You Need Your Own Small Army, and Who's Got Your Back

Maybe you're not ready to head off to the ends of the earth to spend four years working for free, but if you've read this far, you probably have at least one big goal you are committed to achieving over a long period of time. No matter the goal, you'll likely discover that you're going to need some help along the way. If you want to become a working artist, you'll need fans and patrons to support you. If your plans involve

> The price of greatness is responsibility.
> —WINSTON CHURCHILL

some kind of entrepreneurial project, then you'll need a group of loyal customers to ensure reliable income over time. Even highly individualistic goals, like writing a book or visiting every country in the world, can benefit greatly from the support of a small army of loyal partners.

Why will people willingly follow you? Because they'll believe in your cause, and because your work helps them in some way. In fact, if you give people a good enough reason, many of them will stick with you for life, allowing you to scale up your project or move to another goal after you achieve the first one. In this chapter we'll look at how to acquire a network of allies and followers, how to make their lives better, and how to put them to work so they can help you at the same time. This chapter examines each part of the process, but first, an important disclaimer.

> **Disclaimer:** I'm going to use the terms "leader" and "followers" here, but I want to be clear that the relationship is not always one-way. Leadership has little to do with titles and everything to do with influence. If you're a leader, never forget that your followers are real people who have a lot to contribute. Wherever your leadership journey takes you, always remember that your followers are not just a number.

A small army typically consists of five groups of people who connect with you in different ways. **Prospects** have heard about you and are curious about what you're doing. Before making any commitment, prospects look for the "reason why"—why should they care? Why should they be interested in what you have to offer?

**Followers**, the largest part of the team, learn of your cause, find it intriguing, and actively seek out more contact from you. If you have a website, they'll join the newsletter list and follow it regularly. If you have a business, they'll buy from you regularly. They are also following a number of other individuals and organizations, so you do not have their exclusive attention—but they care about you and are eager to learn more. They have crossed over to your side of the fence.

**True fans** are hyper-responsive followers. They typically represent 2 to 4 percent of your follower base, and they are completely committed to your success. True fans scream at concerts, go to sports events even when the team is in last place, post comments on blogs, and eagerly watch for any news from their hero. When a musician puts out a new album, her true fans will buy it without waiting for the reviews. In fact, if you have any kind of business, true fans will buy almost everything you sell.

**Allies** are like-minded individuals who are actively waging campaigns of their own in similar fields. They are your peers. Some of them may be followers or true fans of your work as well, but you're both on a similar journey.

Lastly, **friends of friends** represent your extended network. The idea is that when you need specific help with something, you may not necessarily know who to ask—but someone you know can probably help find the right person and connect both of you.

Note that these categories are not completely distinct from one another. You can be a follower, for example, (or even a true fan) and also be an ally. People will also sometimes move between one category and another as they interact with you and everyone else who is connected to their lives. Instead of thinking too much about categorization, it's more important to spend time on recruiting and maintaining your small army—and then putting them to work.

## The Plan of Action

Most recruitment and maintenance activities for your small army fit into these three steps:

Step 1: Recruit Your Small Army

Step 2: Train and Reward Your Army

Step 3: Ask Your Army for Help

Each step is related and in some cases may occur simultaneously, but let's break it down a little for simplicity's sake.

### STEP 1: RECRUIT YOUR SMALL ARMY

Between email, text messaging, social networks, traditional media, and offline interactions, there is no shortage of messages competing for our attention. To stand out from the crowd, you'll need a platform to speak from, a good reason why people should pay attention to you, and a welcoming environment that encourages prospects to get involved.

### THE PLATFORM

Before you do anything else, you're going to need a platform where you can address your small army. At the battle of Agincourt, the army of Henry V was able to defeat the French despite being vastly outnumbered. According to Shakespeare, the rout began after King Henry jumped up on the back of a hay cart to make an impromptu platform for an inspiring message. Despite fighting in the mud against an army five times larger, the "band of brothers" won a lopsided victory in large part because of King Henry's creative use of a platform to speak to the troops.

Thankfully, modern-day armies do not require the use of hay carts, nor do they need to fight many live battles in the mud. Since the introduction of the Internet, platforms usually consist of different kinds of websites and the careful development of a mailing list. Websites can be blogs, forums, podcasts, social networking profiles, or something new. The most effective communicators use two or more of these methods to speak to followers in different ways.

## THE REASON WHY

After you've created a good platform, you'll want to put out your shingle and let the world know you're looking for help. The people who learn of your work and stop by to check it out are your prospects, and they won't stay prospects for very long. With all of the other messages competing for their attention, most prospects will make a quick decision on whether they want to stick around for a while or return to the other distractions.

To move prospects from window shoppers to followers, you'll need to focus on asking and answering the "reason why." The "reason why" refers to the question we all ask when we check out a new person, organization, or even a general resource such as a book or website. The question is: "Why should I care about this?" or, phrased differently, "What's in it for me?"

In the English language alone, there are now more than 110 million blogs being regularly updated. Why should someone care about yours or mine? Besides the fact that we can get any book we want through an Internet retailer, the average bricks-and-mortar Barnes & Noble stocks 120,000 books. Why should we pay attention to any particular one of them? If you can turn the tables and look at your project with this kind of brutally honest thinking, you'll quickly see whether or not you provide a good "reason why" your prospects should become followers. If the answer is discouraging, you don't need to give up—but you should probably revise your strategy.

When I first decided to create a website to chronicle my journey to every country in the world, I showed the initial concept to a few friends. All of them thought it was interesting, but one of them immediately applied the "reason why" thinking. "It sounds fun," he said. "But what does it do for someone like me?"

His question bothered me, because aside from fellow adventure travel junkies, I couldn't think of a good reason why anyone else would be interested in my goal. As I thought about it further, I realized that I had to do more than just write a diary of my adventures around the world. The website I eventually developed included the travel essays, but also a number of other topics focused on achieving big goals and creating a life of personal freedom. With freedom as the primary goal, my followers could travel like I do—or they could pursue something else that was more meaningful to them. Without the better answer to the "reason why" question, the project might have been interesting, but not tremendously helpful for anyone other than me.

## THE WELCOMING ENVIRONMENT

You want people to feel encouraged by participating in something greater than themselves or in something that connects them with others. Your message should be "Come join me. Be a part of something bigger than yourself. There are other people who see the world in a similar way."

That's the kind of message that caused me to move to Africa and work for free. It's also the message that shifts us from interested prospects to becoming followers or true fans of any interesting individual or organization. The same inspiration comes about through products and services that bring significant value into our lives.

However, you'll need to be careful about something. As prospects check you out, take the time to make sure you're converting the right people to followers and true fans. Don't make the common mistake of believing that "everyone" is a potential recruit for your cause. Not only are some people a poor match for your audience, some will do more harm than good. The wrong people will drain your energy, distract you from what is important, and may even try to influence you to give up.

Who are you trying to reach with your message? Remember, it can't be "everyone." The target market defines who is *not* part of your audience as much as it defines who is. Clearly tell prospects who you are looking for, and tell them that you're not going to be like everyone else out there. For example, Ron Paul attracts libertarian-minded citizens who believe the federal government should be eliminated or significantly reduced. There aren't many people who think Ron Paul is just "okay." Having a mission statement like Ron Paul's is a good way to attract the followers you want while deflecting anyone else.

Putting forward controversial opinions from time to time will also help you gain a following and filter out prospects who aren't a good match. There's an old joke about the president who asks for a one-armed economist because he is tired of his advisors giving their opinion and then saying, "Well, on the other hand." The point is that refusing to present a real opinion is always the safe road. Instead, take the road of risk by taking a stand.

## STEP 2: TRAIN AND REWARD YOUR ARMY

Once you have provided a compelling reason for people to pay attention and begun to convert prospects to followers, you'll want to deepen the relationship. You do this by meeting the needs of your army and helping them get what they want. To better illustrate this idea, consider two things that are inherent in any group of followers: motivation and rewards.

### THE MOTIVATION

Why do you read the books you do and listen to certain musicians or bands? Why do you visit certain websites over and over? Chances are because you are somehow motivated by what you learn or experience. If you stop being motivated by someone you follow, you might give them another chance or two, but sooner or later you'll stop paying attention. Other attributes may be optional, but motivation is mandatory.

Motivation comes in three forms: inspiration, education, and entertainment. When deciding how to train your army, you'll need to choose from these three forms or create your own combination of them, based on who you are and what your goals are. A combination of two or three forms of motivation is usually best, but of the three, inspiration is the one that will keep your army coming back.

This is where you as an individual have an advantage over large companies or other organizations: you can be yourself. You can show the failures and successes on a personal level. Leo Babauta has done this to near perfection on his popular blog *Zen Habits*, where he writes about simplicity and goal-setting. In less than a year, Leo built a subscriber base of more than 100,000 avid readers and became a full-time blogger.

Many of these readers were attracted to Leo's humble presentation of himself as an average guy yearning to live a healthy, simplified lifestyle. The educational component of Leo's writing is important (some of the top posts include "10 Tips for Quitting Smoking" and "30 Days to a Flat Stomach"), but the inspirational, personal side of *Zen Habits* is even more of a draw. I don't smoke, but when I first discovered the site, I read Leo's post about quitting smoking out of curiosity to see how he had made the change. Even if I don't learn something from Leo's site every day, I'll usually feel somewhat inspired after visiting. That's why I continue to go back, and I suspect many other readers feel the same way.

## THE REWARDS

When it comes to rewarding your army, you can keep your checkbook in the drawer. However, followers and true fans still like to be rewarded in other ways—usually through the work you do for them, regular communication, and as much personal recognition as is practical. If you don't pay an army for a while, it tends to mutiny, or—even worse—stop paying attention to you.

One early December morning, I opened up a small box from UPS. "Funny," I thought. "I don't recall ordering anything this week." Inside the box was a new iPod—a thank-you gift from a commercial printer I had used several times that year. I also received a number of holiday cards from other vendors, but the printer was the only one who sent me an iPod. You can probably guess that my loyalty to that company went way up after receiving the unexpected package.

You don't need to send iPods to your entire army (although that would certainly be impressive), but if you can provide other kinds of unexpected rewards and recognition, you'll strengthen the relationship between you and your network. Author Jack Canfield suggests that you write three personal notes or thank-you letters every day. Some might consider this advice outdated now that most people use email, but actually the opposite is true. A personal note, especially one that is unexpected, will almost always create a real impact on the recipient.

The key principle is to go beyond the expected. I don't pay much attention to holiday cards from vendors, but a small business that sends me an iPod definitely exceeds my expectations by far. Similarly, an online reader who writes an offline card brightens my day more than any email could have.

## STEP 3: ASKING YOUR ARMY FOR HELP

Only after you have attracted prospects, converted them to followers or true fans, and deepened the relationship can you ask people to really help you. Technically, you can ask for small things in the beginning—join the email list, confirm your subscription, complete a survey, and so on. To go beyond the basics, though, you'll need to have established a strong relationship and proven that you are worth helping on a more significant level.

When you're ready, what can your army do for you? How can you ask them for help or put them to work? Let's look at five different ideas.

### OPTION 1: HELP YOU SPREAD THE WORD

The most basic, entry-level commitment a follower can make is to help bring in new prospects to your campaign. Followers have their own circles of influence, and they can get the message out to the people they know far more effectively than you ever could on your own. When they endorse your work or personality, their own friends and followers will pay attention.

If you are a writer, you can ask readers to help spread the word about your books, stories, articles, or blog posts. Be specific—not just "Please tell someone about this," but "Please pass this on to three other people" or "Please submit this post on your favorite social network." If you are a visual artist who relies on galleries or coffee shops to show your work, ask everyone you know for contacts in the industry. Use the "weak ties" phenomenon (discussed on the next page) to your advantage by finding out how you can get in touch with galleries that are more prestigious than you would otherwise feel comfortable approaching on your own.

If you are a speaker, teacher, or consultant, you probably know that the best thing you can do is get some experience under your belt so that companies and event planners will hire you. Even as a beginner, you can do this by letting your small army know you are available. You may need to work for free at first, but once you get a few events under your belt and have good references, you can go back to your network and ask for more help finding paid opportunities.

## OPTION 2: HELP YOU CONNECT WITH ANYONE

As part of asking for help, you'll also want to connect with the fourth and fifth groups of people in your network, your allies and friends of friends. Remember that allies are on a journey similar to yours. The challenges they face will also be similar— and they'll likely know a number of other people in the field that you haven't met yet.

You should connect with potential allies as early as possible. When you launch a new project, actively introduce yourself to everyone who has influenced you and anyone in a similar field. Tell them what you're doing and how their work has been an inspiration. Help them out wherever you can without keeping score. Don't try to sell them on anything or ask for something at this point; instead, aim to establish a relationship.

One of the most interesting facts about social networking is that most people love to introduce and connect other people. Perhaps most interestingly of all, the people known by your followers may end up being more helpful than the people you know directly. This is because of the social phenomenon known as the "strength of weak ties." See the "Online Resources" section of this book for more info, but all you really need to know is that "weak ties" refers to *people unknown to you but known to your friends and allies.*

Strong Ties = People you know directly

Weak Ties = People known to your network (friends of friends)

The interesting thing is that even though the people known to your network are referred to as "weak ties," when you're referred to them by a mutually trusted friend, the relationship is instantly strengthened. As you recruit your small army, chances are someone you know will know exactly how to help you meet anyone else you need to know.

## OPTION 3: PROVIDE FINANCIAL SUPPORT

As you build a small army over time, your followers can financially support your work even if your primary goal is to do something different than run a business. In a popular online essay, former *Wired* magazine editor Kevin Kelly argued that it is possible for a musician, band, or almost any artist to earn a good, sustainable income with a fan base of just 1,000 true fans. Remember that a true fan is someone who will buy almost anything you produce. These fans will drive long distances to concerts, actively post reviews of your work, debate critics on your behalf, and regularly tell their friends about you.

This model is an evolution of the classical arts tradition, where individual artists were supported by patrons who appreciated their work. Back in the day, an artist might have only one patron who agreed to support him in return for artistic dedications and commissioned projects. The beauty of the small army model is that with a number like 1,000 fans, the artist is not dependent on such a small source of support. Some fans will inevitably drop out throughout the life span of an entire career, but if artists can maintain a suitable base, their financial support need not suffer and can even grow over time.

## OPTION 4: GROW YOUR BUSINESS

When run properly, a small business will attract prospects, customers (fans), and hyper-responsive customers (true fans) over time. Once you have acquired a sufficient base of each group, there are a number of things you can do to leverage the relationship to grow your business.

With the support of the true fans of your business, you can create a continuity program to increase monthly income. You can build a funnel of entry-level products that lead to higher-level products, enabling you to serve customers who are at different stages in their relationship with you.* Most important, you can aim to redefine the conversation between you and your customers by taking the emphasis away from selling and toward meeting the needs of people who look to you for help and inspiration. Instead of selling products, you focus on solving problems. Instead of attracting skepticism, you build trust.

For a good example of how this works, consider the interesting model of public radio and TV stations. If you ever listen to public radio or watch public television, you probably know that the content is freely offered without advertising. Once or twice a year, the station will conduct a fund-raising drive where gentle (or not-so-gentle) social pressure is used to convince free riders to join the paying subscriber group—a direct application of converting prospects and followers (listeners) to true fans (contributors).

This model can now be adapted on a micro level thanks to the widespread adoption of the Internet. Some creative entrepreneurs are discovering that they can do essentially the same thing with their own network of followers and fans: give everything away without restrictions, and ask the small army to decide what to pay. Since most of us can't easily open a new public radio station, let's look at two examples of individuals who have succeeded by adapting this model to different mediums.

---

* Information on how to create a continuity program and build a product funnel is available through the "Online Resources" section of this book.

### Example 1: The Travel Writer

David Rowell runs *The Travel Insider*, a website and email newsletter about the airline industry. Each Friday since November 2001, David has sent out a long, detailed message summarizing what has been happening in the airline world that week. The newsletter is highly opinionated—some readers get upset about David's rants—but over time, David has benefited from his "tell-it-like-it-is" reputation and built a core following.

All of the content David offers his readers is free, but since this is his full-time job, naturally he needs to be supported. Once a year, David produces a fund-raiser where he asks readers to contribute. A core group of about 800 subscribers typically responds to the call for help, contributing a range of amounts from very small ($5 to $10) to $250 or more, with $50 being the average. For the rest of the year, David is relatively silent about his need for support. Additional contributions do come in from time to time, but the bulk of his yearly income is derived from contributions and pledges made during the fund drive. These true fans, and a number of general followers, are happy to "pay" David for the free newsletter he sends them each Friday.

### Example 2: The Online Comic Strip

From a small storefront office that contains more video game consoles than computers, Mike Krahulik and Jerry Holkins design a triweekly comic strip filled with inside jokes that is read by hundreds of thousands of video gamers. The tone of *Penny Arcade*, their comic strip, is frequently lewd, and sometimes the inside jokes aren't even understood by the insiders. Mike and Jerry would be the first to say that the humor of *Penny Arcade* isn't for everyone. Instead, it is for their own small army.

In the beginning, Mike and Jerry admitted that they enjoyed making the comic strip but had no idea how to run any kind of business. This was not a crucial problem in the early days, but then they started hosting video game conventions for a few thousand of their closest friends. Going from online comic strip to worldwide gaming convention wasn't easy. They needed an army, and they found one in their massively loyal fans, who volunteered in huge numbers to staff the convention and keep the peace. In 2007 they moved out of a local conference center into the enormous Washington State Visitors and Convention Center in downtown Seattle.

In addition to the gaming conventions, *Penny Arcade* has also utilized its vast network to help children's hospitals throughout the United States and Canada. They do this through an annual fund-raiser called Child's Play. Since 2003, the army of gamers has raised more than $2 million in donations for toys and games at children's hospitals, proving that a subculture not always regarded as being outwardly focused (predominately male video game players) can rise to the occasion of a good cause.

## OPTION 5: JOIN THE CAUSE, LITERALLY

Once you go beyond the basic commitments, you can also ask followers to literally join you on location to advance your cause. This requires a greater commitment than most followers can make, but that's okay—if you have a worthy cause and have built the right relationships, the people who are a good fit won't hesitate to sign up, while other followers can cheer the rest of you on from the sidelines.

When it comes to asking people to literally join your cause, the possibilities extend from the significant to the fanatical. Dean Karnazes, an ultramarathon runner who gained fame for having pizza delivered to him on the street while running through the night, set a goal of running 50 marathons across the United States in 50 days. The idea was interesting by itself, but fortunately, Dean and his sponsors had the good sense to think carefully about the *reason why* other people would care about it.

To answer the question and provide a good reason, Dean decided against the original idea of running each marathon by himself on unofficial courses. Instead, he would run each race on a registered course with other runners who had signed up in advance to come out and join him. On some days, more than 50 solo runners, including a few who had never run more than 10 miles at one time before, came out to run the entire 26.2-mile event with Dean. Together they raised money for charity while boosting the awareness of running all across the country.

Gary Parker, the California surgeon who had been living in Africa for 17 years, offered me a chance to join his cause on location. I eagerly embraced it, and many others did too. One of the others was 30-year-old Scott Harrison, a former nightclub promoter from New York City who had grown tired of partying every night and was looking for a more meaningful commitment. As what he originally viewed as "a year of penance," Scott joined Gary and me in Benin to document the work of the organization and learn more about international development.

When the year was up, Scott was ready to move back to New York—but he didn't want to promote parties anymore. This time, Scott decided to promote the need for clean water and sanitation throughout Africa. From his days as a nightclub promoter, Scott had amassed an email list of 12,000 people. Many were personal friends, others were colleagues, and others were models and celebrities. Instead of starting over, Scott decided to start with the list. He wrote to everyone he knew and told them his idea, founding an international charity that donated 100 percent of revenue directly to program expenses. The money would fund local charities in the neediest countries in the world, and to provide accountability, they would use images from Google Earth that proved when the wells and latrines had been installed.

Presented with the compelling story and a way to help, Scott's small army of nightclub contacts came through. Relying primarily on volunteers and a few staff members funded by grants, Scott built Charity: Water to a $5 million organization in less than three years. The organization's volunteer board of directors is responsible for paying Scott's salary and funding the administrative costs of the organization, while Charity: Water continues to give 100 percent of its income directly to field partners.

## WARNING: HOW TO DEFEAT YOUR OWN SMALL ARMY

It all sounds so simple. Recruit people who care about your work enough to support you, provide them with continual motivation to follow along, and then charge off to storm the castle. Well, that's basically how it works, but if it's that simple, why doesn't every artist, entrepreneur, or anyone else with a big goal follow this model?

First, understand that it is not easy to get a significant number of followers and true fans. You can follow lots of people (I keep up with about 100 email lists and blogs), but you can only be a true fan of a few. Next, trust is hard to gain but very easy to lose. If you want to destroy the relationship between you and your followers, all you need to do is abuse their trust. To defeat your own small army, simply don't do what you say you're going to do, and don't apologize when you make a mistake. If you let people down without explanation or apology, good luck rebuilding that trust.

Unfortunately, avoiding this blunder is harder than it looks. No one starts a campaign to change the world with the idea that they will end up letting people down. The problem usually comes about when the project is succeeding rather than failing. When things are going smoothly and you find you can take shortcuts that no one seems to notice, you may be tempted to take more and more shortcuts. Eventually, *everyone* notices, but by then it may be too late. If you want to maintain the momentum and keep your followers happy, don't give in to the temptation.

In short, your goal as a leader is to challenge people without insulting them. You want to lift up your followers and improve their lives in a meaningful way. If you continue to meet the needs of your fan base, it won't be difficult to maintain their trust. When you can do that and are willing to keep working for a long time, your army will succeed, and so will you.

*   *   *

What do comic strips, international charities, travel writers, ultramarathon runners, musicians, and small businesses have in common? To help them succeed, all of these campaigns recruit a small army of followers. They help followers get what they want, and they convert followers into true fans. They leverage relationships with allies and friends of friends to bring them the needed connections and resources.

Remember that our lives are connected with other people all over the world. By identifying a specific cause and recruiting a small army, you can achieve far greater success than you otherwise could on your own. Cultural anthropologist Margaret Mead once said something that has been repeated in graduation ceremonies ever since: "Never doubt that a small group of thoughtful, committed citizens can change the world. Indeed, it is the only thing that ever has."

Margaret Mead was right. Your small army can help you achieve your own goals. They can help you help others. They themselves will be helped at the same time, in true win-win-win fashion. What are you waiting for?

**REMEMBER THIS**

- Think carefully about how you can help people get what they want. If your campaign uplifts others or meets an important need, you're on the right track.

- Create at least three ways your followers can connect with you—examples include a blog with RSS feed, a profile on a social networking site, a newsletter, or a live event.

- Communicate in at least two mediums. For example, if you are a writer with a blog, supplement the written posts with an occasional podcast or video message.

- Directly ask people to join your army, and then ask them for specific help.

- Set a target goal: within the next x months I will have x new followers in my small army.

CHAPTER

# The Personal Finance Journey

I'd like to live as a poor man, with lots of money.

—PABLO PICASSO

Adam and Courtney Baker, 26 and 25 years old respectively, had been married a year and were settling into life in Indianapolis. They settled in so well, in fact, that they quickly found themselves with an outsized portion of debt. In addition to $50,000 in student loans, Adam and Courtney had two car loans, another loan from their parents, several credit card balances, and even a line of credit at the jewelry store.

Irresponsible? Maybe, but it also wasn't that unusual. Courtney had a stable job as a teacher. Adam was running a profitable property management business, in between hosting poker tournaments on the side that brought in an extra $100 an hour in spending money. No one questioned them about taking on all the debt, and since they were able to make the minimum payments each month, it didn't seem like a problem.

The birth of their daughter Millie served as an effective

catalyst for change. Adam had been working 80 to 100 hours a week in the business, a practice he realized wasn't sustainable. Poker tournaments were fun, but the lifestyle didn't suit a family guy. Both Adam and Courtney had also begun thinking about the future and looking warily at the debt they had allowed themselves to accumulate. They decided to make a big change—and the sooner, the better.

To deal with the debt, Adam and Courtney published a personal "declaration of war," promising to rein in the spending and get serious about savings. For 18 months they buckled down hard, living on a third of their $60,000 combined income and using the rest to pay down the bills that had gotten out of control. At the same time the war on debt was taking place, Adam and Courtney were also looking at the bigger picture. Eliminating debt was important, but they also knew it wasn't the final goal. They wanted to see the world, and what better time than the present?

"We knew if we stayed in central Indiana another year, we'd never leave," Adam told me. "It wasn't the most logical thing in terms of having just had a kid, but for us it was right."

When it comes to uprooting your life and moving around the world, a lot of people are prone to saying, "I'd do that if we had the money," or "That would be fun if we didn't have a mortgage." Adam and Courtney wanted to show that it's possible to pursue a big dream even if you're not rich. To take the process further, they published an online list of everything they owned, then they moved with one-year-old Millie from Indianapolis to New Zealand for a year of living abroad. The emphasis on careful budgeting continues, and their website includes a section they call "radical financial transparency" where they list 100 percent of their monthly expenses—but the war on debt was only the beginning to the full life that the whole Baker family is now embracing.

## Money, Life Planning, and Happiness

To state the obvious, personal finance is personal. Just as you shouldn't let anyone else determine your goals and values, you should also seek to maintain control over your own financial priorities. More than almost any other aspect of identity, if you don't have clarity of purpose over how you view the role of money in your life, you'll likely end up going along with what other people do.

The typical objection to the life planning exercises that we looked at in the earlier chapters is "That's nice, but how do you pay for all of that?" I think this objection stems from general skepticism about people who live intentionally. If everyone is jumping off the bridge, you're going to attract attention by coolly looking over the edge and carefully considering whether you really want to leap.

The most important part of unconventional life planning is to be clear on what you want. As the Cheshire Cat said in *Alice in Wonderland*, "If you don't know where you're going, any road will take you there." Applied to living on your own terms, if you don't know what you really want, how will you know how to get it?

The second reason why defining a clear direction is important, regardless of how much money you have, is that we often discover that the life we want is in closer reach than we initially thought. As discussed in chapter 2, most of us don't really want to retire to spending every day on the beach or keeping the servants busy in a European castle. Instead, we want a meaningful life filled with the right kind of work and plenty of time to do other things we enjoy.

Despite the likelihood that you don't actually want the private jet and the castle in Switzerland, it's true that life costs money. You might as well understand exactly how much you need, how much you'd like to have, and what you'll do with it when you get it. As for me, I've made as little as $8,000 a year as a student (and then about $12,000 a year as an aid worker), and as much as $250,000 a year as an entrepreneur during a couple of good years. I can tell you from experience that my happiness level was not significantly different when comparing the $8,000 years and the $250,000 years. Some things are certainly easier with a lot of money, but other things become more difficult.*

Mae West famously said, "I've been rich and I've been poor. Believe me, rich is better." She was right about not being poor, but the correlation between money and happiness only goes so

---

* When you make a lot of money, you tend to worry a lot more about losing it. These days I earn somewhere in the middle of the extreme range of $8,000 and $250,000 a year. In my "279 Days to Overnight Success" report, I outlined exactly how much money I earn from my personal website. You can download it for free at ChrisGuillebeau.com/overnight-success.

far. The amount of income someone needs to be happy is highly personal and varies by geographic area, but studies have consistently shown that there is a relatively low limit beyond which happiness and income are not directly related. To take one estimate, after a person earns around $40,000 a year, the amount of happiness doesn't increase very much. The goal is to know where *you* fall on the money and happiness scale, so you can then plan your life accordingly.

## FRUGALITY AND SPENDING

I embrace frugality as a personal value, but frugality for me is not about pinching pennies in every part of my budget. Instead, it's about making conscious choices to spend on the things I value—and avoid spending on other things. After paying the rent and other recurring bills, the way I approach my discretionary spending is outlined below.

1. I happily exchange money for things I truly value.

2. As much as possible, I don't exchange money for things I don't value.

3. All things being equal, I value life experiences more than physical possessions.

4. Investing in others is at least as important as my own long-term savings.

Travel is my biggest personal expense, and I regularly spend about 20 percent of my annual income on it. Many people spend 20 percent or more of their income on debt reduction, and I've taken great care to ensure I have no debt. If I can't afford to pay for something in full, I don't buy it.

In addition to big expenses like round-the-world plane tickets, I also appreciate the privilege of spending small, regular amounts of money on things I particularly enjoy. I like going to Thai or Mexican restaurants for lunch and having a coffee break at Starbucks or a local shop in the afternoon. I don't eat out every day, but after I achieved enough regular income where I *could* go out for lunch whenever I wanted, I felt happy.

This is where my practice of frugality differs from conventional interpretations. My view is that if you like having a latte every morning and feel like the purchase is a good value, by all means pick up a morning latte. It's much more important to worry about eliminating debt and being clear about the bulk of your spending.

While I purposely plan for round-the-world tickets and don't mind going to Chipotle several days a week, I'm adamantly opposed to exchanging money for things I *don't* value. In my case, I don't feel the need to have a car, and I purposely relocated to a city where public transit is affordable and reliable. I also spend only about $100 to $200 a year on new clothes.

Admittedly, there are a couple of exceptions to the rule of paying only for what I value. I don't have much choice over paying the electric bill, for example, but I want to make sure I'm not paying a whole set of electric bills each month. I also don't like paying $400 a month for a health insurance policy that doesn't cover doctor's visits, but because I am self-employed and living in the United States, it's just what I have to do. Yes, it bothers me, but after a few running injuries for me and an ankle surgery for Jolie, I don't think it would be wise to attempt to be uninsured as long as we live in America.

Aside from the necessary exceptions, I'll work hard to ensure my spending is aligned with the overall values I've chosen. The next one is that I generally prefer life experiences to "stuff." Stuff represents things that fill up the house, while life experiences represent things that I *do*. Concerts, long weekends in nearby cities, dinners with friends—those things are experiences. Clothes, household items, and pretty much anything that takes up physical space falls into the stuff category, which I'd prefer to avoid or at least limit.

Lastly, because I know I've received a lot from life thus far, I want to make sure I actively give back in the form of investing in others. Each of these ideas is discussed in more detail throughout the next section.

## A FEW PRINCIPLES

I'm going to offer a few personal finance suggestions here, but the key is to be deliberate in your own value judgments. I don't necessarily think my way is best for everyone, but I also know that many people experience a great deal of internal dissonance over where they spend their money. No matter how you decide to manage your money, it greatly helps if you're clear about your values.

**Time is not money.** I embrace frugality partially as a means to an end, but it's also a personal value. Being frugal in some areas allows me to spend freely in others. It's not always a direct relationship, though—my decision not to pay $2 to ride the bus home from an appointment one day doesn't allow me to buy a $4,000 round-the-world plane ticket. Under a strict "time is money" perspective, it would be much better for me to ride the bus home (10 minutes) than to walk (30 minutes). The incongruity doesn't bother me, because it's not my goal to live the most optimized life possible. The key is to avoid doing things out of habit or because I'm not brave enough to overcome my fear of change (see chapter 3).

**Deferred gratification can be a form of life avoidance.** Deferred gratification, the principle of sacrificing something now in hopes of enjoying it in the future, has both pros and cons. I'm writing this book a year in advance of publication, giving up other income and devoting a lot of time in hopes that you'll eventually read it, all because I believe in the project. I also deposited $300 in my long-term savings account this month, another sacrifice I was happy to make.

At the same time, the practice of deferred gratification can also serve to help people avoid making a lot of decisions about how they actually live now. This is one aspect of my financial life where I definitely want balance—I don't mind saving for the future, but not at the expense of enjoying life today. What if you save for 40 years, putting off all kinds of opportunities, then get hit by a bus the day before retirement? Better to plan for the future while also living in the present.

**There is no such thing as good debt.** I realize there is a debate over whether some kinds of debt are "good" versus other kinds that are "bad." "Good debt" usually refers to student loans or mortgages, whereas "bad debt" refers to credit card debt and other high-interest loans. Personally, I don't want to owe anyone anything. Even the so-called good debt locks people into decisions that they may not be comfortable with for all of the years they hold the debt.

For years I stated my preference for renting instead of owning a home, and it was clear from the conversations that I was almost always in the minority. These days, I'm happy to see more and more people beginning to understand that a 30-year mortgage isn't always in the homeowner's best interest. I'm also glad that the housing market has tightened up and it's much harder for people to get mortgages where the repayment schedule is a high proportion of their income.

**To get serious about saving, focus on increasing income more than cutting expenses.** This is because cutting expenses is essentially a scarcity behavior, whereas increasing income is essentially an abundance behavior. As an entrepreneur, I have a certain amount of control over my income. If I want to make more, there are a number of projects I can take on to increase revenue. I realize this is tricky, because I like to save money and eliminate unnecessary spending too—so we'll look at this distinction more in the next chapter. The point is that it may be easier to increase income, especially for those who are inclined to self-employment.

**Work toward financial independence, but never retire.**

## ESCAPING DEBT ASAP

If you're already in debt and want to escape, you can do one of two things: (1) find a way to pay it back, as quickly as possible, or (2) look for an alternative solution like deferral or debt forgiveness in exchange for public service.

Check out Adam Baker's site at ManVsDebt.com for an interesting profile of someone pursuing the first option. Sean Ogle, profiled in chapter 3, waged his own war on debt by spending virtually all his disposable income on paying back his credit cards and car loan. (Then he got even more serious and sold the car.)

By the way, if you're in debt and looking for the way out, you're not alone. A broad community of personal finance bloggers from every conceivable demographic have set up their own sites to share tips and strategies for whittling down debt and embracing frugality. The kingpin of these blogs is GetRichSlowly.org. Many other sites can be found by checking out *Man Vs. Debt* or *Get Rich Slowly*.

Lastly, you may need to sacrifice or put a few things on hold to bring the debt under control—but as Adam's and other stories show, you don't have to postpone your entire life just because you're in debt. It's at least as important to enjoy your life as it is to escape the debt.

Retirement for many of us is an old-fashioned idea—we may want to retire from a particular job and then move on to something else, but we don't necessarily want to stop working altogether. In my early days of goal-setting, I decided I wanted to be financially independent. I originally defined this as having enough wealth to be able to live off the interest without doing any other work in exchange for money.

As the next couple of years went by, I reevaluated this goal and began to see that my definition was a bit too traditional. Since I never wanted to formally retire, why was it so important for me to accumulate a large amount of capital? It would be better, I realized, to focus on creating financial security through an income-based strategy. Let's look at the difference.

## WEALTH-BASED FINANCIAL INDEPENDENCE
## (USUALLY A $1M+ TOTAL GOAL)

Financial experts love to argue about these things, but the consensus allows for a 4 percent withdrawal rate on your total financial assets every year. This means that to achieve wealth-based financial independence, you'll need to save roughly 25 times your expected annual expenses. For example, to be able to safely withdraw $40,000 per year, you'd need to amass $1,000,000 in savings. For $100,000, you'd need to have $2.5 million. You'll also need to account for expected inflation, since $40,000 now won't be worth the same $40,000 years later.

## INCOME-BASED FINANCIAL INDEPENDENCE
## (USUALLY A $100K OR LESS ANNUAL GOAL)

Income-based financial independence is based on replacing employer income with self-created income. Instead of trying to accumulate *wealth* (all the money you have in an investment account), you think primarily about increasing and diversifying *income*. The goal here is not so much to save a big fortune, but to change your sources of revenue to the point where you can regularly obtain enough income without working for an employer.*

Instead of making the accumulation of wealth (capital) my goal, I decided to focus more on building my income in a manner that would allow me to do almost everything I wanted without the confines of a day job. I also moved away from the pursuit of wealth to goals that were oriented more toward life experiences. I wanted to build a business, but I also wanted to travel. I chose to sacrifice some of the wealth-building for the travel, giving up additional income so I could embrace other, more rewarding experiences.

"Full" financial independence in the form of accumulating a large amount of capital is still a valid goal, but I've come to see it in the "nice work if you can get it" category. Since I have all I need to live on, and don't feel like I have to make a lot of sacrifices in the things I care about the most, I'm not that worried about it. It will happen eventually, and in the meantime, I'll be enjoying the life I value most.

## Using the Power of Your Purse to Help Others

Just as money is a tool to help you get what you really want—remember, it has no value by itself—it can also be a tool to help

---

* As discussed in chapter 5, whether you continue to work a "real job" or not is a different question.

other people acquire the same freedom. Every year I try to contribute to my long-term savings fund, but I also make a number of investments in non-profit organizations based on a percentage of my income. My goal is to give 20 percent or more, but for transparency's sake I should note that I haven't been able to meet this figure every year. It's always been at least 10 percent, though—the "tithe" is the threshold I set up on an automatic deduction from my bank account to make sure I don't fall too far behind.

I call this principle "investing in people." I'll use the words "giving" and "charity" here because they are more commonly understood, but I want to be clear that I don't view this principle as an act of generosity; I view it as an act of responsibility and gratitude. I've made a lot of things happen for myself, but I'm not blind to the great privileges that come from being born in a rich country. I also recognize the numerous social privileges that allowed me to make relatively free and open choices. Where much is given, much is required.

If you're wondering what this has to do with non-conformity, I'd say that non-conformity is all about making choices differently. If you live in poverty, you don't have the luxury to make as many choices—or to put it another way, those who are poor have very little freedom. Helping people to increase their own freedom and opportunities is a natural response to the recognition of freedom in our own lives. Giving money isn't the only way to help, of course, but it's an important way that should not be minimized in a consideration of personal finance.

When you're thinking about investing in people for the first time, you may wonder where to get started. I especially appreciate charities that focus not only on raising money, but also on connecting donors with the ultimate beneficiaries of the charity's work. To that end, the AONC book and website is actively supporting a Charity: Water project in Ethiopia. If you're not sure where to start your investing in others, I'd love to have you join our cause. In fact, if you've purchased this book, you've already helped with a small contribution. Learn more at CharityWater.org/aonc.

> If we command our wealth, we shall be rich and free; if our wealth commands us, we are poor indeed.
>
> —EDMUND BURKE

I'm naturally excited about the project I'm involved with, but a few other organizations that are worth investing in are also listed below. None of these organizations are political or religious; they are focused strictly on reducing poverty, empowering small business owners, or otherwise strengthening the infrastructure of countries and communities around the world.

**Partners in Health:** Founded by Dr. Paul Farmer, this organization is at the forefront of public health issues in Haiti, Africa, and elsewhere. Find them at PIH.org.

**CARE:** I especially respect CARE for several courageous choices the organization has made in recent years to turn down funding that was tied to inefficient, outdated development practices in Africa. Learn more at Care.org.

**Kiva:** Giving to Kiva is more like loaning money to a friend, with a 98 percent guarantee that you'll get the money back. Learn more at Kiva.org.

**Oxfam International:** Oxfam is a conglomerate made up of 13 smaller organizations divided by country. Collectively, the goal is to end poverty and injustice by 2012. I suspect they'll need to extend the goal, but to even make good progress, they're going to need some help. Find your local office at Oxfam.org.

**Doctors Without Borders:** This organization, known around the world by the French name *Medecins Sans Frontieres*, brings medical teams to war zones, natural disasters, and countries that lack sufficient health care. Learn more at DoctorsWithout Borders.org.

> It is pretty hard to tell what does bring happiness; poverty and wealth have both failed.
>
> —KIN HUBBARD

Instead of making a one-time gift, it's usually better to make an ongoing monthly commitment to an organization you like, even if the gift is small. Most international development organizations receive the bulk of their funding only when disaster strikes, and a monthly gift will help them receive reliable income even when the world's attention isn't on them.

One final tip about giving: when you give, let go. There's an old joke about a street musician who approaches a well-dressed man and asks for a dollar to buy a drink. The man gives him the dollar, but then hesitates. "Hey, wait a minute," he says. "How do I know you won't take this and spend it on food?"

You probably don't want to devote a big portion of your investment in people toward buying vodka for street musicians, but the point is that you're not responsible for what happens after you give. Most of the time I prefer to give to trusted organizations because there is greater accountability with the funds, but in the end, what they do with the money is up to them. Once you give, let it go. It's literally out of your hands at that point, and that's where it should stay.

When I first started writing about my ideas, I published a number of guest articles for other blogs. A friend in Portland, J. D. Roth, was kind enough to host one of the articles on his great personal finance site, GetRichSlowly.org. I got a lot of good feedback from the post—that's when I started receiving all the notes about students who regretted taking on loans—but I also got a fair amount of critical feedback as well. One of the comments, reproduced below, was especially insightful:

> I have enough money to last me the rest of my life, unless I buy something.
>
> —JACKIE MASON

I'd really love to see what Chris's life is like when he's too old to work. I hope all his memories of traveling the world and giving his money away comfort him when he's eating dog food in a shared-living facility for the indigent.

I sent that comment out to my family and a few friends. We laughed about it, and someone suggested I print and frame it in my office. As bizarre as it was, the more I thought about it, the more we realized that "dog food man," as my friends called him, was partially right. I hope my diet will be a bit better than what he suggested, and I hope I get my own room in the indigent house, but I won't really be surprised if I'm comforted by my memories. What else do we have at the end of our lives?

Let's close this chapter with the words of D. H. Lawrence: "Life is something to be spent, not saved." I agree.

**REMEMBER THIS**

- Money and happiness are correlated to a certain degree, but not much after that.

- Your behavior with money has to match up with your overall values.

- Consider "investing in yourself" through spending on unique life experiences more than "stuff."

- A good savings program also includes investment in others. It's not about guilt; it's about gratitude.

# INTERLUDE

## WHAT THEY SAY ABOUT WINNERS

Hugh MacLeod, full-time artist and author of *Ignore Everybody*, explained it like this: "If you want to make a lot of people hate you, all you need to do is make a lot of money doing something you love." You could also replace "make a lot of money" with a number of other phrases that reflect success:

". . . all you need to do is have a lot of fun . . ."

". . . all you need to do is help a lot of people . . ."

". . . all you need to do is be better than everyone else . . ."

One thing's for certain: when you set out on an unconventional journey, you'll attract attention and criticism. If you succeed in your quest, you can expect more of both.

Some people enjoy nothing more than putting down winners. I call them energy-sucking vampires—they don't contribute anything positive to the world, but they enjoy lashing out and attempting to suck the life away from other people. Their worldview comes from a perspective of scarcity, where winning and losing is viewed as a zero-sum game. Just because you're winning does not require someone else to lose, but not everyone understands that.

People who possess self-confidence and focus are often labeled as arrogant by those who lack both qualities. According to the scarcity perspective, winners are viewed with suspicion because they "must have" taken something from someone else on their rise to the top. It's easier to bring winners down a notch than it is to rise to their level.

"Great spirits have always been violently oppressed by mediocre minds," reported Albert Einstein, who was said to be mentally slow and incurious as a child. Here are a few other things that have been said about winners:

"Lance Armstrong is embarrassing the tour."—Head of the Tour de France on Lance's return in 2009

"Coldplay is the most insufferable band of the decade."—*New York Times*' Jon Pareles

"We don't like their sound, and guitar music is on the way out."—Decca Recording Company, rejecting the Beatles in 1962

"The grotesque scribblings of a child have a naiveté, a sincerity which make one smile, but the excesses of this school sicken or disgust."—Emile Cardon on Monet, Renoir, and the other Impressionists

It's good to be aware of the things people say, but that doesn't mean you have to let them stop you from pursuing your goals. When you start to attract vampires, congratulations: you're well on your way. Just don't give in. The rest of us are counting on you to keep going.

# PART III

# The Power of Convergence

Let's put it all together. Work, adventure, and building a legacy that will far outlast your time on the planet. If that sounds good to you, jump on in.

# Radical Exclusion and the Quest for Abundance

*Every man dies; not every man really lives.*

—WILLIAM WALLACE

My favorite novelist is Haruki Murakami, who has essentially created his own genre of work. In Murakami's books, cats talk to people, fish fall from the sky, entire worlds of alternate reality are created, and all kinds of other crazy things happen. The protagonists usually spend a lot of time wandering around Japan and doing whatever they feel like, which strikes some readers as boring but is one of the main reasons why I enjoy Murakami's novels so much. (I also spend a lot of time wandering the world without an agenda.)

After 30 years of writing fiction, Murakami published a nonfiction book that explained his writing process and philosophy. One of the most interesting points was when Murakami discussed a choice he had made at the beginning of his career. Having completed his first novel shortly after turning 30, Murakami set out to prioritize the greatest part of his life to be spent developing a relationship with a wide group of readers who followed his work over time. Here's how he put it in his own words:

> I placed the highest priority on the sort of life that lets me focus on writing . . . I felt that the indispensable relationship I should build in my life was not with a specific person, but with an unspecified number of readers. As long as I got my day-to-day life set so that each work was an improvement over the last, then many of my readers would welcome whatever life I chose for myself. Shouldn't this be my duty as a novelist, and my top priority?*

We tend to read statements like that and immediately dismiss them as unrealistic, or perhaps even rude. How could someone choose to prioritize their relationships with countless people they had never met? Shouldn't Murakami focus on his family, close friends, and local community first—and then in his spare time, worry about the people who read his novels?

> Learn from yesterday, live for today, hope for tomorrow.
>
> —ALBERT EINSTEIN

Another way to look at it is that Murakami focused on what he would gain instead of what he would lose. He identified what he really wanted and ordered his life around that.

---

* Haruki Murakami, *What I Talk About When I Talk About Running* (New York: Knopf, 2008).

The practice of abundance, which we'll focus on in this chapter, is all about embracing life to the fullest and ordering your life around a few key priorities. To make that happen, you'll need to look carefully at all of your current obligations to determine which ones are actually necessary and which can be eliminated.

## It's Not a Paradox

This chapter ties together two conflicting ideas and shows how it is possible to take on a broad range of activities while also simplifying to the essentials. I appreciate the concepts of simplicity, decluttering, and minimalism, but I think of them in the same way as frugality: I want to connect them to a greater purpose related to a life of abundance. I want

> Ambition is not a vice of little people.
>
> —MICHEL DE MONTAIGNE

to shut some things out while letting other things in. If you've ever come back tired from a vacation, if you've ever used the phrase "working for the weekend," or if you've ever wondered about the elusive life/work balance idea, maybe it's time to think more about convergence.

As we'll consider it here, convergence is the *state of being where everything in our lives is in alignment.* We have good relationships with family and close friends, we're excited about work, we're in good health, we do more or less what we want to every day, and we know we're making a difference in the world. In short, we find ourselves full of gratitude and regularly challenged in an active, abundant life. To achieve convergence, two separate (but related) activities are required: saying goodbye to unnecessary tasks, obligations, and expectations—then welcoming in a wide range of other things that enrich our lives.

## Part 1: Eliminating the Unnecessary

As Murakami found, setting the terms of an unconventional life begins with an active decision. If you want to take on the world and live life your own way, you'll need to be fairly determined, because there will be no shortage of distractions that crop up every day. These distractions include:

- The 3,000 marketing messages that most of us take in every day

- Busywork given to you by others or that you create for yourself

- Unnecessary obligations or responsibilities

- Social norms and widely held beliefs about work and time (the belief that you must work a certain number of hours each day, for example—without considering what actually gets accomplished during that time)

When you're starting to redefine how you spend your time and you're not sure which responsibilities you should commit to, it can be helpful to begin to apply a filter to all the inputs that come your way. Asking two questions—"Why should I do this?" and "What will happen if I don't?"—will clarify a great many responsibilities for you.

> *Example:* You have a meeting coming up that you know will be unproductive.

> *Ask:* "Why should I do this?" (Possible answers. I'm supposed to go, it's just what we do every week, something could be different this time, etc.)

> *Ask:* "What will happen if I don't attend?" (Possible answers: Probably nothing, someone may be irritated, someone else may think I was smart to skip out, etc.)

If the answer is that you'll be immediately fired, you may need to suck it up and go to the meeting. But chances are, you can probably find a way to skip the meeting and still live to see another day.

In fact, if you want to get serious, you can take the question even further when you encounter something you don't want to do. "Will the world end if I don't do this? Will someone die?" Assuming the answer is no, you can safely place the commitment in the unnecessary column. You may still end up doing it, but you'll have given yourself an out that allows you to back away if you prefer.

As you begin to implement this practice, you'll gradually learn to discern necessary from unnecessary obligations. The next step is to say no to as many unnecessary obligations as possible. Saying no is critically important for setting the terms of your life, and the further you advance toward your personal goals, the more you'll have to decline requests for your time. You may even need to devote extended periods of time to what I call "radical exclusion," or shutting out absolutely anything that serves as a distraction from your key priorities.

> The great secret of success is to go through life as a man who never gets used up.
>
> —ALBERT SCHWEITZER

Radical exclusion is more a state of being than an activity, although it can be helpful to set aside a specific block of time for it. When you go into this phase, you strive to limit the number of new inputs to your life so that you can focus on a specific project or brainstorming session. Bill Gates famously did this during his "Think Weeks," where twice a year he would shut out all distractions and head into a room of reading material for several days at a time. An aide would bring in grilled cheese sandwiches and diet soda twice a day, and Gates would plot the future of Microsoft's world domination strategy. At the time, he was the richest person in the world and the active CEO of Microsoft, so if he could find the time to back away from the world, I humbly suggest that you and I can do so as well. In fact, I'd suggest a *correlation* between Gates's radical exclusion and his success.

Fair warning: when you choose to limit inputs and withdraw

## THE TO-STOP-DOING LIST

An important principle of life planning is that you can have anything you want, but you can't have everything at the same time. To be able to devote most of your time to projects and activities you enjoy, you'll need to be forceful about dropping a lot of other activities.

The best way to stop spending time on unnecessary distractions is to make a "to stop-doing list." This is better than a to-do list, because it helps you see what's bringing you down. Your to-stop-doing list is exactly what it sounds like: a list of things you simply don't want to do anymore.

Think about the tasks that drain your energy without contributing to anything worthwhile. There will always be tasks that drain your energy for outcomes you believe in—it takes a lot of energy to be a social worker, for example—but the to-stop doing list is for tasks that bring you down without giving you joy or helping anyone else.

Try to come up with at least three to five things you currently do that drain your time and keep your focus away from more important tasks. The first time I made a to-stop-doing list, I realized that I was spending at least five hours a week on things I derived no value from. While life is filled with some things we don't like to do, the principle is that many of these things can be left undone or removed from our weekly activities without much repercussion.

from social requests, not everyone will understand this behavior. Some people may get frustrated with you. Meanwhile, you'll be getting more done and doing more things that you like than all of them.

## LIVING WITH 100 THINGS

In addition to unproductive tasks and wasted meetings that bring us down, the amount of physical "stuff" we have can also limit our potential. Case number one in this exhibit is David Bruno, a writer and entrepreneur who was approaching the end of a business project he had worked on for five years. The business had started on the back of a Starbucks napkin and grown to the point where he sold off his interest and went back to writing and working on websites full-time.

David was troubled with what he viewed as excessive consumerism in America, and he worried about its effect on his own life. To address the concern, he started a personal "100 things challenge." For at least one year, David committed to living with only 100 items in his possession. Since David's 100 things challenge was his own, he made his own rules. "Books" counted as one item even though he had a substantial library, and "socks" and "underwear" counted as one item each even though he kept several sets of each.

David published his 100 things list online and invited others to join him, although he made it clear that it was a personal project he was doing for his own benefit. He described the project as "my little way to personalize my efforts to fight consumerism."* Despite David's hesitance about asking others to join him, it didn't take long for the 100 things project to spread on Facebook and among the blogging community.

I didn't adopt David's 100 things rule completely, but I liked

---

* David's 100 things challenge is posted at GuyNamedDave.com.

the idea enough to start looking around my apartment for things I didn't need. Even though I have a stated aversion to "stuff," I realized I had let a lot of things creep up on me since returning to the United States after living overseas. Why did I need to keep an old computer I hadn't used in months? Why two printers instead of just one? I probably wasn't going to become a professional Guitar Hero player, so why did I still have a plastic guitar with fretboard buttons sitting in the corner?

I decided to pursue an active decluttering strategy. For at least one month, I'd get rid of five things a day. I didn't place any restrictions on the five things, and I didn't care how I disposed of them—some would be given away, some would be donated to the Salvation Army, and others would be discarded in the recycling or trash bins. The more I moved things away from my physical space, the more I found myself able to concentrate on my work and other enjoyable activities.

J. D. Roth of *Get Rich Slowly* fame made a similar rule with his personal wardrobe. One January he moved all of his clothes out of the hall closet and into a guest room closet. Whenever he got something out of the guest room closet to wear, he moved it back into the hall closet. Over the course of a year, most of his favorite clothes made it back to the original closet, but there were still a lot of items remaining in the guest room. The rule was that if he hadn't worn anything in a year, he would donate it to a thrift store.

Giving things away often produces a reluctant "But I might need that later" response, but when the clothes hadn't been worn in a year, the feeling was hard to justify. As an interesting side benefit to shifting the main part of his wardrobe out of the hall closet, going to hunt through the guest room closet felt like going to the mall—except everything was free.

## CHOICES, INPUTS, AND OBLIGATIONS YOU CAN USUALLY END

We've looked at eliminating "stuff," but let's get a little more serious. Why not stop making commitments to events, activities, or people who bring you down? I know that some will consider this harsh, but I try to avoid spending much time with people I find to be negative or who otherwise attempt to subtract value from my life. I know that I probably can't change their behavior, but there's a chance they'll influence me to be more negative than I'd like, just by my being around them.

The same is true with the information we consume. Try turning off the TV for a month, and see if you really miss something important. If anything you read, including this book, is not interesting and helpful to you, you should put it down and spend your time in a more meaningful way. Apply this strategy militantly, and you'll see positive changes in your life almost immediately.

Thinking about what to exclude from a life is like defining an ultimate goal or set of best practices: it's highly personal, and your answers will likely be different from mine. Just as we've done throughout the book, though, I'll offer a few suggestions for your consideration.

**Give up meetings and TV.** Seth Godin writes the number one business blog in the world, with a readership base of hundreds of thousands. He is frequently asked how he has time to do everything, especially write back to everyone who emails him. His answer is that he doesn't watch TV and doesn't go to meetings, so that gives him four to five more hours a day than most people have.

**Give up the phone.** Use the phone for people you want to talk to and ignore the rest. Check voicemail once a week, if at all. To be fair, your voicemail message shouldn't say, "Leave a message and I'll call you back." Do you really want to call everyone back? If not, just leave a message with your name.*

Contrary to conventional wisdom, you can do this in business too. I decided a long time ago to stop chasing customers. I do post a phone number on my business websites, but in most cases the number goes directly to an automated recording that tells callers to use the website for support. When customers request personal help by phone, I tell them, "Sorry, but due to my frequent international travel, I do not provide phone support. I understand if this means you won't buy something from our company."

This practice was incredibly freeing. A few people have complained over the years, but I've made the policy as transparent as possible. Interestingly, some of the people who complained and

---

* My friend Crystal recorded a message on her phone that says, "Hi, this is Crystal. I don't like voicemail and only check it about once a week. If you need to reach me, feel free to send an email to _____@gmail.com."

said they wouldn't shop from a merchant who did not have a real phone number ended up buying anyway.

**Give up email.** Personally, I like email, so I don't want to give it up. But if email stresses you out or you find yourself unable to keep your eye off your inbox, it's not a necessary part of life. Leo Babauta from the popular blog *Zen Habits* recently gave it up, and he used to send and receive up to 300 emails a day.* If you're getting overwhelmed, you can also declare "email bankruptcy" and start over from the beginning. To do this, take a deep breath, hit the "Archive" button on all your mail, and send the following message to your contacts:

> Subject: I've declared email bankruptcy
> Dear friends, family, coworkers, and spammers,
>
> Your message is important to me, but I'm getting overwhelmed. There are currently xxx unread messages in my inbox. It freaks me out every time I look at it.
>
> To fix the problem, I've decided to "go bankrupt" and start over. I've archived all the old messages and won't be trying to sort them out. The good news is that I'll be more attentive from now on.
>
> Thank you for your understanding.

(Sending the message is optional, but if you're really worried about missing something important, you might want to consider it.)

---

*Leo does admit to having a "secret" email address, but the 300 messages a day have dropped to less than 30.

## Part 2: Enriching Our Lives Through Abundance

The acts of decluttering and radical exclusion raise the question of what should stay. After you banish unnecessary or undesirable things from your life, what do you *keep*?

I propose welcoming in a life of abundance, filled to the brim with things you enjoy doing and that leave a legacy. We'll look at legacy more in chapter 11, but it starts with living a full life. At the end of the day, I want to be tired—not from a grind of tasks that leave me with a feeling of "What did I really do today?" but with a sense of *wow*.

Let's go back to some of the things we looked at in chapter 2: the life list, the ideal world, the goals. Don't you want more of that, not less? How can we get more? Believe it or not, part of it starts with stress—the good kind. As best illustrated by Mihaly Csikszentmihalyi in his classic book *Flow*, the moments in life we are most proud of can actually be stressful:

> The best moments in our lives are not the passive, receptive, relaxing times . . . the best moments usually occur when a person's body or mind is stretched to its limits in a voluntary effort to accomplish something difficult and worthwhile.

As for me, I'm interested in finding out what I can accomplish with the whole 168 hours available to all of us each week. Subtract sleeping hours, and you get a more realistic 98 hours a week. Subtract a Sabbath day, which we'll look at in a moment, and you get 74 hours. That's 74 hours, or 4,440 minutes, to fill with things you like to do.

I don't want to waste those minutes. I want to run marathons, start businesses, build websites, write, talk with fun people, help non-profits, travel to 20 countries a year, and sometimes sleep. Have I mentioned I drink coffee? I like coffee.

I know from experience that if I *didn't* do these things, I'd be miserable. Whenever I sit still for too long, I feel like my brain is atrophying. I'm interested in reducing useless, unnecessary stress, but when given the choice to do something interesting, I want to find a way to make it happen.

## UNDERSTANDING HOW YOU RELAX AND RECHARGE

I think it's best to spend the majority of our weekly 4,440 minutes on meaningful projects and relationships, but you'll also want to understand how you best relax. As an introvert, I generally find this time by myself. Especially when I'm traveling in a faraway place where I don't speak the language, I sometimes go days at a time with very few interactions. Sometimes these days can be lonely, but I don't think loneliness is always a bad thing if it allows us to slow down and reflect on the world around us.

When I'm not traveling, I try to take a Sabbath day every week from 6 p.m. on Saturday to 6 p.m. on Sunday. During that time I'll be 90 percent offline, which means I may log on to read the weekend newspapers, but I won't be hitting my email or working. Otherwise, any time for work or fun is fair game.

## AVOID THE PARADOX: KNOW THE DIFFERENCE BETWEEN YES AND NO

When you encounter opportunities, distractions, and requests for your time, how do you decide whether to say yes or no? It's up to you (as always), but here are a few ideas:

- Say yes to legacy work. (We'll look at this much more in chapter 11.)
- Say yes to work that leaves a deliverable. (Define work in output instead of time.)
- Say yes to your kind of fun.
- Say no to work that doesn't leave a deliverable (unnecessary meetings).
- Say no to busywork.
- Say no to things you would do only out of obligation.
- Perform an instant gut check: yes or no? If you have a bad feeling about something, say no. If you feel slightly intimidated but also excited, say yes.

\* \* \*

How is it possible to dramatically reduce certain inputs while simultaneously increasing the amount of other inputs and activities? The answer is that doing less of some equals doing more of something else. You can have almost anything you want, but you can't have it all at the same time. ("Anything but not everything" is how productivity leader David Allen puts it.)

Practicing the art of radical exclusion is good for two reasons: first, it eliminates the unnecessary from our lives. But just as important, when you say no to some things, it gives you the chance to say

yes to many more. All things being equal, I'd rather regret something I did than wish I had done something (but sat it out due to
fear or other commitments). Let's embrace more of life, not less.
Balanced people don't change the world, and I'd rather spend my
time feeling worn out from meaningful activities and projects.

How about you? After sleeping and a day of rest, how will
you spend your 4,440 spare minutes this week?

### REMEMBER THIS

- You can probably have anything you want, but probably not
  everything at once. Radical exclusion is the process of eliminating things that are unnecessary, or even stepping away
  from almost everything for a set period of time.

- Creating a to-stop-doing list can usually help eliminate several hours of tasks in the average week.

- Asking "What's the worst thing that can happen if I don't
  do this?" may help you feel better about eliminating an
  obligation.

- After eliminating the unnecessary, start opening up to everything you've always wanted to do. It's not a paradox; it's a life
  of abundance.

# 10 | Contrarian Adventures

Through travel I first became aware of the outside world; it was through travel that I found my own introspective way into becoming a part of it.

—EUDORA WELTY

I got in the back of the group taxi in Beirut, Lebanon, and passed over $8 to the driver's sidekick in the middle seat. "Damascus?" I asked again, just to make sure. He nodded, took my money, and we set off—me, a couple of Canadian travelers I had met up with at the taxi stand, and half a dozen Arabs who had family members across the border.

Getting a visa for Syria from the consulate in California had required a fair amount of hassle. I dutifully sent in the application along with the $75 fee, but it took several weeks of phone calls—and one additional payment, in cash—before the consulate officer finally relented. I received my passport and a bright green visa for Syria the day before I left for the trip, which began with a week of bouncing around South America before continuing over to the Middle East.

Getting the visa was stressful, but over at the Lebanese-Syrian border, the atmosphere was calm and even friendly. Contrary to what I had read before leaving, I discovered that I could have received the visa at the border crossing for a third of the price, without having to send off my passport to an unknown office and hoping for the best. The border officials waved me through, and to my amusement we passed by a Dunkin' Donuts in the no-man's-land between countries. I was up for grabbing a cup of coffee and a bag of Munchkins for the road, but the rest of the passengers had already cleared immigration and were ready to go.

When we arrived at the bus stop outside Damascus an hour later, the Canadians and I looked around at the numerous taxi drivers who gathered to bid for our business. Choosing one who seemed especially helpful, we made it to the famed Old City, checked into a hostel, and spent the rest of the day exploring markets and mosques.

Over the next couple of days I worked in an Internet café and on the roof of my terrace from 9 in the morning to 1 p.m., stopping for lunch and a walk around the city. In the late afternoons and evenings I spent time with my new friends and several Syrians we had met on the first night. At the end of the week I reluctantly said goodbye and headed for Amman, Jordan, where I'd catch a flight over to Asia and eventually head home. It was sad to leave the road, but I knew I'd be back a few weeks later. Going to a place like Syria could easily be a once-in-a-lifetime adventure, but for me it was just another day at the office.

## A Nomadic Education

I've always liked maps. When I was a kid, I spent hours combing through atlases, working out driving routes across the United States, memorizing the capitals of every country, and dreaming of faraway places. I was fortunate to have several early cross-cultural experiences that helped me appreciate the similarities and differences of people in faraway parts of the world. I was born in Virginia but grew up in several different places, including Montana, Alabama, and the Philippines. My parents lived in different parts of the country, so at least twice a year I'd be sent off as an unaccompanied minor to make the trek on a series of flights. After a few trips I knew the airports in Atlanta, Minneapolis, and Salt Lake City better than any other ten-year-old, and I enjoyed deliberately losing my assigned escort and wandering around the concourses on my own.

> Travel is the only thing you buy that makes you richer.
>
> —ANONYMOUS

When Jolie and I moved to West Africa in 2002, I became even more comfortable traveling to different places. During our final two years overseas, I served as the programs director for Mercy Ships, the medical charity we had first heard about after 9/11. Part of the job required me to hopscotch around the region, meeting government leaders, inspecting ports, and touring clinics.

On one flight from Sierra Leone to Guinea, I saw a bottle of water duct-taped to the wall and labeled "Fire Extinguisher." Thankfully, we didn't have to use it. On another flight to the Ivory Coast, our small, ancient turboprop plane was already beginning to taxi down the runway when an African guy in a suit came running along beside, frantically trying to flag us down. To my surprise, the plane stopped and allowed him to board—after he stuffed a fistful of money into the copilot's hand.

The trips were physically hard but emotionally stimulating. I was regularly asked for bribes, I learned to speak French while being detained at the presidential mansion in Guinea, and I had to fend off malarial mosquitoes while sleeping in missionary guesthouses on the beach at night. I didn't love the mosquitoes, but everything else was enthralling.

After a year of that kind of travel, I was ready to explore more of the world. One trip was scheduled to take me from Liberia to Benin (in West Africa) and then down to Johannesburg (in South Africa). Because flight options within Africa are limited, I figured out that it would cost less to fly from Benin to Europe and *then* down to Johannesburg. Since it was a long trip, I arranged to take a couple of personal days in Europe before continuing on to the next stop.

I had been in Europe several times before, but only in countries like France and Holland, and never on a solo trip. When the travel agent booked the flight, I discovered I could get to Budapest for the same price as landing in Paris. Perfect. From Budapest I traveled to Prague on the train, and the six-hour journey gave me plenty of time to reflect on all the places I had been so far.

I started counting up all of the countries I had visited and saw that the total was around 50. "Not bad," I thought, "but what would it take to get to 100?" When I started breaking it down into time and financial cost, I realized it would cost roughly $30,000 and several years of regular travel to get to the next 50 countries. I was stunned at how relatively little it was. My friends at home were buying cars (usually SUVs or minivans at the time) that sometimes ran upward of $30,000. My time living overseas had given me a new appreciation for simplicity and frugality, so I had no desire to spend that much money on a car. Choosing to see the world, however, was an investment I could easily buy into.

After I returned to the United States and started going to graduate school, I used every break between terms to fly overseas. During the first year, I went to places as varied as Burma, Egypt, Kosovo, Moldova, and Uganda. The more I traveled, the more comfortable I became, and the more I learned about what I call "travel hacking"—my system of using round-the-world fares, a big stash of frequent flyer miles, and other tricks to bring the cost of my trips down to around $400 per flight anywhere in the world.

As mentioned way back in chapter 2, the fun thing about setting big goals is that once we really get serious about setting them, we often find that they take less time to achieve than we initially expect. For my 100-country goal, this was certainly the case. On one of the early trips I booked a "Circle Pacific" ticket, which allowed me to visit several countries in Asia from the United States by arriving via the north (China, Korea, or Japan), swinging through the region on a couple of stops (Vietnam, Hong Kong, Singapore), and going home through the south (Australia or New Zealand). On my second stop in Hong Kong, I took the ferry over to Macao, another Chinese territory. While riding along for an hour, I dug out my old notes on the 100-country quest. By then I had made it to about 80 countries, and it was less than two years from when I had first set the goal at 100.

> For my part, I travel not to go anywhere, but to go. I travel for travel's sake. The great affair is to move.
>
> —ROBERT LOUIS STEVENSON

That's when the thought hit me: instead of limiting the goal to just 100 countries, why not go to all 192? For the rest of the ferry ride, I tried to map out what it would look like and how long it would take. One of the things that separates a goal from a dream is a deadline, so I gave myself until my thirty-fifth birthday—just under five years away at the time. The whole time I walked around Macao, my head was spinning. Could I make it to all 192 countries? What if something went wrong or I ran out of money?

After talking with my family and thinking about it for a few weeks more after returning home, I decided to formally adopt the quest. Depending on when you read this, I'm either still under way or coming down to the final, difficult years. I've been to a lot of interesting places recently—Syria, Iraq, Pakistan, Mongolia, Swaziland, among others—but going from 100 to the full 192 gets progressively more difficult due to the nature of hopping from place to place.

My home is now in the Pacific Northwest, but home is just where I live in between roaming the rest of the world. I also feel at home in parts of Asia, Africa, and Europe. I realized recently that I'd accomplished an important goal I had never formally set: virtually the whole world had become open to me. I can now arrive in countries I've never been to before, and instinctively know how to get around and figure things out. I also experience a sense of homecoming in numerous places I return to frequently on each continent.

If the nomadic life is something you're interested in, I also believe the world can become fully open to *you*. This isn't just about globalization, although the fact that some of us live in a flat world definitely helps. It's also about everything else we've looked at in the book so far— how to do what you want and relentlessly focus on what matters to you.

## What If Travel Isn't Your Thing?

This chapter focuses on seeing the world, and I know that not everyone wants to see the world in the same way. Some people may not be interested in frequent travel or worldwide relocating at all. Remember, this is just what I do. I include the example of contrarian adventures for two reasons. First, to show what's possible when you work toward creating your desired lifestyle. I'm self-employed but not independently wealthy, and I don't have any unfair advantage that isn't obtainable to most of the people who will read this book.

Second, even though not everyone likes to travel, I've noticed that when you ask, "If you could do anything, what would it be?" one of the most frequent answers is "I would travel more." There are many variations on the kind of travel any particular person aspires to—some of us would backpack through Southeast Asia, others would trek to Hawaii in search of perfect surfing, still others would look for some kind of volunteer vacation in Africa or Latin America—but the point is that the desire to travel frequently rises to the top of many "If I could do anything" lists.

Because not everyone likes to travel the same way, I call what I do "contrarian adventures." My particular style of travel uses the principles shown throughout the book: there is almost always an alternative way to accomplish something; you should do what you want instead of what others expect; and the goal is to achieve as much convergence as possible around everything you are passionate about.

If you really don't like anything about exploration, you can safely skip the rest of this chapter. Be careful, though: I've found that even people who say they don't like travel can usually think of at least one place somewhere in the world they'd like to visit before they die. I believe that if you can save as little as $2 a day, you can get to that place within two years or less. Many places cost less, and if you can save more than $2 a day, you can get there sooner. Unless you're certain that you don't have any interest in the outside world, you might as well consider a few options for venturing beyond your immediate surroundings.

## How to See Experience the World

If you're new to world travel, the experience can be intimidating. How you choose to set forth is as much a result of your own personality and style as anything else.

**Thoughtful planning.** The planner is an engineer who takes the time to map everything out in advance. If you're expecting me to criticize this approach, I'm not going to. Whenever I've been stuck somewhere because of my own stupidity or poor planning, I often wish I had used the engineering approach. Since I usually tend to wing it, you'll have to do your own thoughtful research on thoughtful planning. It probably involves guidebooks, spreadsheets, and double-checking to make sure you actually have a plane ticket for the place you plan to visit.

**Test the waters.** The concept of mini-breaks has become popular in part due to Rolf Potts's *Vagabonding* book, Tim Ferriss's popular *4-Hour Workweek,* and the general subculture of digital nomads who work from anywhere. Web developer Cody McKibben took this approach when he moved to Bangkok, Thailand. He bought a ticket from California, received a 90-day visa upon arrival at the airport, and said to himself, "Great! I've got three months to figure out what I'm going to do." His apartment, which he displayed on YouTube to the amazement of his friends in California, cost a bit more than $200 a month.

Over the three months, Cody adjusted to life in Thailand and worked on building a small consulting business. Cody hasn't struck it rich yet, but he doesn't need to. He spends much of his free time helping a local charity, In Search of Sanuk, which was founded by another expatriate friend who permanently relocated to Thailand.

**Jump in with both feet.** Some people become expert planners without ever actually doing anything. To avoid that trap, you can also get a round-the-world ticket or one-way discount fare, pack your bags, head to the airport, and figure the rest out as you go. As long as you pick a relatively affordable destination as a starting point, it's not that difficult. Affordable (and fun) choices include most of Latin America; the subregion of Cambodia, Laos, and Thailand in Southeast Asia; and South Africa.

Gary Arndt, a former software executive, took it even further. "The idea of traveling around the world wasn't something that gradually dawned on me," Gary said. "It all happened in an instant. Once I had the idea, I knew it was something I had to do." He left home, gave away everything that didn't fit into one suitcase, and started traveling alone on an itinerary he decided to fill in later. Two years and 70 countries later, he's still going.

Jeanne and Vince Dee did the same thing, except they brought a three-year-old along with them. Their daughter, now six years old, has become completely bilingual, and the whole family has been traveling nonstop for the past three years. So far the Dees have been to more than 30 countries together, mostly traveling overland on bikes, cargo ships, buses, and other creative modes of transportation.*

## How It Works for Me

The alternative lifestyle I've chosen allows me to travel around the world several times a year without paying a great deal of money. I stay in hotels for free using the many loyalty program points I accumulate through travel hacking (more on that in a moment), on the couches of friends who offer to host me, and once in a while on the floor of the airport before an early flight. Just as work expands to fill the time allotted to it, so too do the possibilities of travel expand as you get more creative and adventurous.

A typical trip for me is two or three weeks long, repeated several times a year to each major world region. During that time, I'll visit several places, usually on at least two different continents. Typically, at least one of the stops will be somewhere I've been at least a few times before, and at least one place will be a new stop for me. Now that I've been traveling for a while, I can get around pretty quickly and I don't struggle with the culture shock that often hits new travelers.

My kind of travel is not about sightseeing or visiting museums. A lot of the questions I'm asked in travel interviews are

---

* Follow Gary Arndt's travels at Everything-Everywhere.com. Follow the Dees, also mentioned in chapter 4, at SoulTravelers3.com.

rudimentary. What kind of backpack do I use? None. What's the weirdest thing I've eaten? I'm vegetarian, so a lot of the "weird" things are off-limits for me. What's my favorite country? I don't have just one, but among others, I really like South Africa, Hong Kong, Macedonia, Jordan, and Chile.

Instead of obsessing over luggage, I like exploring, reading on park benches, and being spontaneous. I don't claim to be an expert on every place I visit, and I wouldn't make a good tour guide. After receiving nearly 1,000 stamps in my passport over the past decade, though, I'm pretty comfortable with settling in and finding my way around almost anywhere.

I simultaneously work and travel at the same time. If I've been staying in hostels or guesthouses, every few days I'll check into a business hotel so I can catch up on the hundreds of emails that I receive every day. If I have an important blog post going up in the morning on the East Coast, but I'm traveling in Asia, I'll set my alarm clock so I can be awake to review feedback the first hour it goes live.

Because I could be anywhere, I try to accommodate the other person's schedule when working on a group project. In Kuwait I slept from midnight to 4 a.m., woke up for a conference call via Skype, then went for a run along the seashore before going back to bed for the rest of the morning. (If you're going to run in Kuwait, where the temperature can be more than 120 degrees during the day, 4 a.m. is a good time to do it.) Sometimes it can be stressful. But I do work from anywhere I am in the world, and for the most part, it turns out just fine for me.

## Highs and Lows

I've done whatever it takes to turn my dream into a workable goal, but it's safe to say that it hasn't always gone well. In Mongolia I was evicted from my guesthouse at midnight when someone else showed up who was willing to pay more for the room. In both Pakistan and Saudi Arabia I was nearly deported for arriving without the proper visa. In both cases, everything turned out fine—but for a long hour in each place, I had the uneasy experience of sitting in an immigration office with a guard next to me, having already cleared departure immigration in the prior stop but not yet admitted to the new country.

The challenges and low moments are part of the adventure, but I have plenty of high moments too. In London's Heathrow airport, I got to hang out for four hours in the Virgin Atlantic Upper Class Lounge. The lounge includes your choice of one free spa treatment, and I opted for the haircut. Naturally, I asked to be seated in Richard Branson's chair. The stylist laughed and said, "You're not the first one to ask that."

In other words, I take the good with the bad. Just as balanced people don't usually change the world, my feeling is that mediocre travel doesn't produce many memories. Bring on the champagne (Virgin Atlantic) and the mosquitoes (guesthouses and long bus rides everywhere). If I have a bad experience or don't like one particular place, I can always go somewhere else.

## TRAVEL HACKING BASICS

This book isn't about travel hacking, and some of the info here won't be relevant for everyone. For those who are interested, however, here are a few of my favorite "travel hacks" that have helped me get around the world. For more info, check out the "Online Resources" section.

- Once you earn elite status with one airline, you can request a "status match" from several others to become a high-flyer on every major airline alliance. (Just be careful, because some airlines only allow one status match per lifetime.)

- If you're stumped with a travel dilemma, visit the forums at FlyerTalk.com. Some of the experts on these boards are even more experienced than I am, and if you ask nicely, several will offer free advice on your itinerary or travel issue.

- If you're looking for lodging and hotel prices are high, check Hostels.com for a large database of guesthouses and smaller establishments. In addition to dorms, many of the properties offer private rooms with breakfast and Internet access. If you're up for company, you can also stay for free thanks to CouchSurfing.com.

- Priceline.com can be a good source for discounted hotels (it's not usually worth it for plane tickets), but the company has an advantage on consumers by not disclosing the minimum successful bids. To negate this advantage, use Google to search for "Priceline winning hotel bids" to find several sites that list the hidden information. I've used this strategy to stay at the Brussels Marriott for $60 (usually $240), the Prague Sheraton for $45 (usually $195), and many other nice hotels all over the world.

- If transatlantic airfare is pricey, look for a repositioning cruise. These cruises take place twice a year as cruise lines move their ships from the Mediterranean to the United States. (A smaller number also go from Alaska to East Asia, and from California to Florida via the Panama Canal.)

- I use round-the-world tickets for most of my long-haul flights. The booking process can take some time to navigate, but if you travel extensively, it's well worth your time to study up. My tickets are usually booked through the OneWorld or Star Alliance airline families.

- Without a lot of effort, most people can easily earn at least 25,000 miles a year without changing any of their spending habits. That's enough for one free ticket—and for those who are up for it, you can spend more time on it and earn up to 100,000 miles without much difficulty.

- When redeeming frequent flyer miles, you can request rewards on partner airlines, and the value is often better than on the domestic carrier. I've used partner rewards to go to Mongolia (Korean Airlines, booked with Delta SkyMiles), Kuwait (Qatar Airways, booked with American Express points), and dozens of other places.

Extensive world travel isn't for everyone, but I wouldn't have it any other way. Portions of this book were written in at least 10 countries. When I got stuck midpoint, I booked a one-way cruise from Los Angeles to Vancouver that was selling at a rock-bottom rate. I spent the day holed up in my cabin and sitting on the deck, jotting down notes for later editing. At one point we sailed under the Golden Gate Bridge while I outlined the next chapter. It wasn't quite as adventurous as an all-night bus ride through Albania (2008) or a flight to Easter Island in the South Pacific (2007), but I enjoyed the setting.

Then when I got home, I plugged back into my online world and started looking for flights to East Timor. Time's running out on my goal, and I still have a lot of places to go.

**REMEMBER THIS**

- Most people have at least one place in their minds they'd really like to go to "one day." By saving just $2 a day, you can usually get there within two years or less.

- Working on location from anywhere in the world rarely involves sitting in the sand with your laptop. It isn't for everyone, nor is it always easy—but for me and many others, it's worth it.

- As with most things in life, if you choose to get serious about travel, you can find alternative ways to accomplish almost any specific goal.

- "Travel hacking" helps to reduce costs and allow for more interesting experiences than conventional travel planning does.

- The kind of travel you value is better than anyone else's idea of fun and adventure. Figure out what you like, and structure your roaming around those preferences.

# 11 Your Legacy Starts Now

> There are certain things that are fundamental to human fulfillment. The essence of these needs is captured in the phrase "to live, to love, to learn, to leave a legacy." The need to leave a legacy is our spiritual need to have a sense of meaning, purpose, personal congruence, and contribution.
>
> —STEPHEN COVEY

I sat in the back of the room as the keynote speaker talked about his glory days as a war veteran. It was a good story for the first five minutes, filled with close calls, bonding with peers, and learning about the outside world as a young man deployed to Southeast Asia in a troubled time.

Then he kept going. He talked for 10, 15, nearly 20 minutes about the war before moving on to the subject he was actually scheduled to speak about. The war in question (Vietnam) took place more than 30 years ago. Yet to hear him talk, it was as if he had just returned from a modern-day tour in Afghanistan. He told the story as if it had all happened yesterday, and anyone listening could appreciate how those months in a war zone had made him into the person he was that day. But it also made me wonder . . . "What has he been doing for the past 30 years?"

I looked around the room. The thing about speaking to a crowd of 200 people is that there are always going to be a few people who love everything you say. Aside from this small group that broke into applause every few minutes, I saw all the other people checking their phones, whispering to their neighbors, or reading through unrelated literature. For the most part, we had stopped paying attention. While our speaker was reliving a war from his youth, we had moved on to the concerns of the present day.

## The Danger of Success

Glory days are dangerous, and while I wish I was immune, I know I'm not. When I came back from Africa in 2006, I made sure everyone knew where I'd been for the past four years. If I met you that summer as I began my new life in Seattle, you'd hear about it within a few minutes of our introduction. Yes, I knew the president of Liberia, and did I mention that Desmond Tutu and I had coffee together one afternoon in Cape Town, South Africa? If not, I'd make sure you heard about it before too long.

It was my story and my identity. I felt deeply proud of those times. As the months wore on, though, I found myself continuing to talk about it with every new person I met. Some of them were interested and wanted to know more. But others, I think, probably cared more about their own life and with what was happening then—just as most of us do.

Those years in West Africa remain an important part of my identity. Much of my formative thinking comes from the many challenging and fulfilling experiences I had during that time. But I gradually came to realize that in a lot of ways, I'd have to leave that time behind and go on to something else.

I began to think about what I was doing next and my goals for the future. Was I going to be talking about West Africa to everyone I met 30 years from now? If so, how would I be different from someone who's still reliving a war that ended decades ago? I could see that I was going to need more than what had already taken place. And if you're serious about making a lasting impact on the world, so are you.

> There are only two ways to live your life. One is as though nothing is a miracle. The other is as though everything is a miracle.
>
> —ALBERT EINSTEIN

## The Best Days of Our Lives

We all have foundational experiences that shape the rest of our lives and determine our worldview. For many of us, these experiences come during high school, college, or university—those years when we feel the most attached to our peers and to the outside world as we view it at the time. For others, the glory days come through a shared experience with a close-knit group such as a military unit or a sports team. Still others find them during an extended trip abroad, at the beginning of a new relationship, or on a job we are especially enamored with.

> Do something wonderful, people may imitate it.
>
> —ALBERT SCHWEITZER

We are rightly proud of our glory days, because they represent a time of rapid discovery and advancement. Looking back, we sometimes refer to them as "the best days of my life." We were challenged and we rose to the challenge. When the time came to an end all too soon, we felt a bittersweet combination of accomplishment and sadness.

But there comes another time, not too long after the glory days have ended, that we need to put them aside and move on to something else. If those life experiences were really so great, shouldn't they provide the motivation for greater challenges? What could the future be like if we applied the lessons we learned and went on to something else that was even better?

When we choose to willingly let go of those times, we're not really saying farewell—we couldn't forget them if we tried. Instead, we say to ourselves, "Wow, that was incredible. I am so fortunate to have had those experiences. Since my glory days were so transformative, I'd better make sure I find a way to have *more* of them somehow."

*   *   *

Here's a novel idea: wherever you are in life, however old you are, begin thinking about every day as the first day of your life. The recognition that all we have is today brings about a combination of good news and bad news. The good news is that the failures have already taken place. There's no need to continue reliving them in your head.

The bad news is that the successes are locked away too. It's fun to look back on them once in a while, but what's done is done—all we have is the present, and hopefully something we can build over time to make a lasting difference in the world. If you like the idea of having more glory days, and you don't want to retire from the sense of being alive, you need to work toward building a legacy. The best time to get to work on it was yesterday. Failing that, today will do.

## The Search for Meaning and the Two Questions

Let's return to the two important questions we looked at briefly earlier: "What do you really want to get out of life?" and "What can you offer the world that no one else can?" Whatever your answers to those questions are, you can likely find the beginnings of your quest to live a full life and make the world a better place for others.

In his classic book *Man's Search for Meaning*, Austrian psychiatrist Viktor Frankl wrote about being imprisoned in a concentration camp for three years. In addition to an extensive journal of his experiences in the camp, Frankl offered a unique theory of meaning and fulfillment. According to Frankl, we find this meaning in one of two ways: "creating a work or doing a deed, or by the attitude we take toward unavoidable suffering."

Hopefully you're not suffering while reading this book, so let's focus on the first path to meaning: creating a work or doing a deed. I call this noble undertaking a "legacy project," and the work we do for it is "legacy work." You may have heard the concept of "legacy" presented as something final. Insurance companies use legacy as a marketing tool, and politicians coming to the end of their terms begin to consider what their legacy will be. When you get old, according to this definition, you look back on your life and think about what its lasting impact will be.

I believe this mind-set is too limited. Instead of waiting, the time to begin thinking about legacy is well before you come to the end of any particular role or life in general. By the time you come to the end, you don't have the chance to change anything that happened long ago. That's why I think it's better to begin thinking about your legacy *right now*, regardless of how old you are or what season of life you're in.

After my time in West Africa was up, I coasted on it for a few months but then realized I would need to move on. I put the photos away and stopped mentioning it to everyone I met. As hard as it was, I needed to find a way to build a new legacy project. For me, the goal was to shift from being a jack-of-all-trades to being a "real writer." I defined "real writer" not so much in terms of income and recognition, but rather as devoting the majority of my creative attention to building a career in writing. The primary motivation was to get my ideas out to people who cared about them. I thought about it off and on for nearly two years, outlining different approaches and trying to figure out what was essential.

> To change is difficult. Not to change is fatal.
>
> —ANONYMOUS

Sometimes you need to reject a number of other, reasonably good choices to create a legacy project. This is because legacy work is different from other good, valid work. Remember the *reason why* question from chapter 7? When it comes to creating a legacy project, you have to apply this kind of analysis even further. In fact, if you want to build something that will provide tremendous value to others and even outlast your own life, you have to be able to clearly answer the question, "How will this really help people?"

Answering this question can be difficult at first because it may cause us to realize how little we do that has any true, lasting value. If that happens, there's no need to be discouraged—remember that "legacy" is something that most people don't consider until they start counting down to the end of something. If you start any earlier, you're well ahead.

When you set out to create something that will outlast you, there are a number of characteristics you need to consider by answering the following questions:

- Vision—how will the world be different because of the project?

- Beneficiaries—who will benefit from the project?

- Primary Method or Medium—how will you do the work?

- Output—what will be produced as a result of your work?

- Metrics—how will success be measured?

As you'd expect, your own legacy project will require your own characteristics. I've listed my answers for the AONC site as a point of reference below, but each project is personal and fundamentally unique.

**Vision:** To empower people to live unconventional, remarkable lives

**Beneficiaries:** A group of at least 100,000 passionate individuals who want to live differently and change the world

**Primary Method or Medium:** Writing (I also create multimedia products and do some limited in-person events)

**Output:** At least two articles each week, one book per year, regular guest columns, 300,000 annual total words (more on this in a moment)

**Metrics:** Site Visitors/Subscribers/Page Views/Social Networking Stats/Nice Emails*

---

* As mentioned briefly in chapter 6, one of the best things about an online writing career is the chance to hear from readers who have made different choices or simply felt affirmed by reading something from the site.

I've used the example of writing because that's what I'm most comfortable with, but there are many other options you can choose for a legacy project. Dr. Gary Parker lives in Africa and does free reconstructive surgery for patients who lack adequate medical care. I think most people would agree that life-changing surgery is an extremely meaningful legacy project. Since it's probably a good idea to get some training before setting out to do surgery, I chose writing instead.

## Legacy Projects Require Legacy Work

When you're building some kind of legacy project, you'll want to focus on doing legacy work. If you're like most of us, every day you'll face some kind of battle between legacy work and busywork. Michael Bungay Stanier, a consultant and business leader, puts it this way: every task and project we choose to spend time on falls into a category of bad work, good work, or great work. We all know we should cut out the bad work as much as possible, but the key distinction is the difference between good work and great work. Good work is useful, productive work. There's nothing wrong with it, but the problem is that *we have too much good work*. Great work, on the other hand, is revolutionary. Great work leads to innovation. While most good work is comforting, great work is simultaneously comforting *and* discomforting because it pushes us to go further.

What Michael calls great work, I call legacy work. The goal

is to move more and more of our work hours away from the busywork category and into the legacy category. On days when I feel like I'm doing at least 50 percent legacy work, I feel good. Otherwise, I have that sinking feeling of having wasted a day I can never get back. I realize that some people may think it's a mistake to base personal well-being and sense of self-worth on productivity. My feeling is: do whatever it takes. If it works for you, don't question it. If not, find some other way to keep yourself motivated enough to focus on the legacy work.

Admittedly, the process of evaluation is usually somewhat subjective. Since I can generally tell when I'm doing legacy work versus busywork, the subjectivity doesn't bother me. If you're a numbers person or want something more measurable, however, you can hack this concept into a more reliable estimate.

Jim Collins, the author of *Good to Great* and other classic business strategy books, is in the enviable position of doing whatever he wants with his time. Naturally, Jim likes to spend much of his time working, but with all the success he's achieved through writing and speaking, that doesn't help to reduce the countless number of opportunities available to him. Because he is relentless about spending a majority of his time on legacy work, Jim carries a stopwatch with him throughout the workday. The stopwatch has three separate timers: one for "creating," one for "teaching," and one for "other." The "other" category is a catch-all for everything that doesn't fit in either the creating or teaching category, and 100 percent of his workday is measured on one of the timers. At the end of the day, the time is logged onto a spreadsheet, with the resulting data posted on a whiteboard.

Jim tracks the rolling average of these three numbers, with the goal of spending at least 50 percent of his time on research and writing, an additional 30 percent on teaching, and the final 20 percent on the remaining catch-all category. Spending only 20 percent of his time on everything not related to teaching or the creative process is a challenge, so that's why he obsessively tracks the metric.

Jim has also learned exactly how much sleep he needs to be productive, so in addition to the weekly work log, he keeps a sleep log as well. If he falls below the required amount over a period of 7 to 10 days, he says, he can still teach and do tasks that fall into the "other" category, but he can't easily create—the most important category of work. Jim maintains this discipline despite many invitations to speak and consult for large sums of money. Instead of going strictly where the money is, Jim accepts only 18 invitations a year, nearly a third of which he provides for free to non-profit organizations. Jim is addicted to living with intensity and building a legacy that will far outlast his life span. Along with coffee (well, at least I think so), this is a good addiction to have.*

---

* I relied on a May 2009 *New York Times* profile of Jim Collins written by Adam Bryant for part of this section.

## GOOD QUESTIONS TO ASK YOURSELF
## WHEN PLANNING FOR LEGACY WORK

In the morning:
- How am I feeling?
- What do I want right now?
- What is the single, most important thing I can do today?

In the evening:
- Who did I help today?
- How much time did I spend creating today?
- Did I move closer to one of my big goals today?
- How much exercise did I do today?
- How much sugar, caffeine, or alcohol did I consume today?
- What do I want for tomorrow?

## Creating vs. Responding

A key principle of legacy work is that it usually involves creating something new as opposed to responding to something that already exists. When you create, you initiate a new project or interaction. When you respond, you're just sustaining an existing interaction. These tips may help you spend more time creating.

**Measure work in output, not hours.** I can sit at a desk and surf the Internet for eight hours, but it doesn't mean I've done any real work. Which is more important—showing up for eight hours or actually doing the work? Believe me, I know very well how to waste an entire workday (I've done it far more often than I'd like to admit). If I were to compile a log of how I spent my time on such a day, it would probably look something like this:

1. Shuffle papers around.

2. Leave Gmail or Outlook open all day.

3. Read the news . . . over and over, from multiple websites.

4. Become upset about an email thread and spend 30 minutes crafting an elegant reply (bonus points for using passive-aggressive language).

5. Rearrange the file cabinet.

6. Pay bills and check online banking.

7. Check up on a few favorite blogs.

And so on. You could probably add to the list, right? Throw unproductive meetings into the mix, which I'm fortunate to have largely escaped these days, and the danger of doing nothing all day is even greater. The point is that none of this work really matters, which is why I like to focus on deliverables (output) instead of hours.

If I spend eight hours staring at the screen and reading the news, the world is not a better place. If I spend 30 minutes working on a project that will add value to my readers or customers, at least some part of the world is better off. My deliverables are articles, essays, product creation, interviews, and so on. An artist's deliverables may be canvases, songs, or something physical. If your work is client-focused, the deliverable is whatever you provide for the client. Whatever your deliverables are, think about those instead of the actual hours you spend getting to them.

**Create a continual metric for your most important work.** In addition to the ongoing commitment to write for my blog readers, I write a newspaper column, weekly posts on several other sites, guest posts for other blogs, freelance articles for travel and business magazines, and lengthy reports that are for sale in my Unconventional Guides business. Each deliverable usually has a deadline that I track in a very simple project management system, but in addition to the specific deadlines, I have a generic "1,000 words" standard.

The 1,000 words standard is that I commit to write at least 1,000 words a day of *something*. I don't necessarily think all 1,000 words are good enough for publication; in this case, the discipline is more important to me than whatever the final deliverable is. I know my own weaknesses, and I know I won't be happy with myself if I miss more than a day or two once in a while. Accounting for Sabbath days and occasional missed days, this allows me to generate an annual output of 300,000 written words—about 100 blog posts, 20 newspaper columns, 20 guest articles for various outlets, 3 information products, and 1 book each year.

One of the reasons this works is because I do a lot of different

## AGE AND EXPERIENCE

A friend of mine likes to say, "Comparison kills." When you start thinking about legacy, it's easy to get hung up on being younger or older than the people you compare yourself to, but the comparison is irrelevant. If you're young and just getting started, good for you. Don't let anyone look down on you because of your age.

If you're older, perhaps you've accumulated some wisdom that came about through the passing of years. Chances are, it's never "too late" to get started on what you secretly wanted to do years ago, and maybe some things will be easier now that you're older.

Personally, I think experience is more important than age. Experience can be acquired at a young age or missed at an older age. Just as there's always someone with more and less money than you, there's always someone older and younger than you. Instead of comparing yourself to others, therefore, keep the competition internal and you won't be disappointed.

kinds of writing. If I only wrote books, I don't think I could sustain that kind of output. The creative diversity definitely helps keep me going. Note also that the editing process inevitably cuts a lot of the initial output. I follow a classic rule of writing and editing: when writing, don't hesitate to include something; when editing, don't hesitate to throw it out. With the average blog post, for example, I'll typically write twice as much as I end up using after a rigorous editing process.

The 1,000-words standard can be adapted to any kind of creative, productive work. A programmer might decide to write 50 lines of code every day, no matter what. A visual artist might do one set of sketches a day. By focusing on deliverables and metrics instead of hours, you'll avoid the bad feeling that comes at the end of a day when nothing has been accomplished.

## But Wait, What About Process?

Isn't the process (or "the journey") more important than the final destination? I tend to think they are equally important. I understand that ultimately the process of doing good work and building a legacy may be more important than the final act itself, but I also think it's good to have a goal. Therefore, I tend to focus on a destination or deliverable, but then immediately move on to a new goal after the first one has been completed. After I finish this book, I plan to write another. I travel for the sake of travel itself; after I visit every country in the world, I don't expect to stop heading out the door. Perhaps it's semantics, but it works for me.

I hope this doesn't contradict everything I just said (Amazon .com reviewers, here is your chance to nail me), but if you're building a serious legacy project, you'll probably need to put in a substantial amount of butt-in-seat time. Sitting down to do something and forcing yourself not to get up until real progress is made can work more powerfully than any time management program. Just be careful about putting in the hours for no good reason, because that's when legacy work shifts back into busywork.

* * *

Regardless of what you've done before or where you are in life now, you can make something beautiful that will outlast you. You can help others in a unique way that couldn't have happened without your influence. That's what a legacy project is all about.

Remember: we all get one life to live. You might as well take it seriously, and a legacy project will ensure that what you bring to the world will continue to be valuable for a long time. Are you up for it?

**REMEMBER THIS**

- All those good things you've done before are nice, but the future can be even better. Focus on that.

- Increase the percentage of legacy work as opposed to busy-work (or even just "good work").

- Setting a continual metric (like the 1,000-words standard) can help keep you focused on what really matters to you.

- Wake up in the middle of the night with good ideas. Share them with the world.

# Dangerous Ideas

Be daring, be different, be impractical, be anything
that will assert integrity of purpose and imaginative
vision against the play-it-safers, the creatures of the
commonplace, the slaves of the ordinary.

—SIR CECIL BEATON

I'm well aware that some of the ideas in this book will not be
eagerly received by a general audience. If you've read this far,
you already know that I'm not interested in reaching a general
audience—but since this book is designed to help you challenge
the status quo, you might as well know how the status quo will
respond.

The most common criticism of unconventional ideas is that
they are unreasonable or impossible to implement. The criticism
is often voiced in statements like these:

"We can't all do what we want all the time."

"Some of us have to be responsible."

"That doesn't work in the real world."

"You wouldn't want a non-conformist heart surgeon, would you?"

"Unreasonable," "unrealistic," and "impractical" are all words used to marginalize a person or idea that fails to conform with conventionally expected standards. My response is that the world *needs* more people who fail to conform and refuse to settle. Without the determined efforts of unreasonable people, most of the rest of us (including the "reasonable" people) would be much worse off. Martin Luther King Jr. was quite unreasonable to suggest that all free men and women in America should be treated equally. Gandhi was quite unreasonable to suggest that India should shake off the chains of colonialism from Britain.

> One can resist the invasion of an army, but one cannot resist the invasion of ideas.
>
> —VICTOR HUGO

Innovation comes from entrepreneurs and others who are wiling to accept risk and try new things. Improvements in social justice come from those who question authority. Being unreasonable or impractical, in other words, doesn't sound that bad to me. That's why I propose an alternative for those who are dissatisfied. Leave the "real world" to those who are happy with it, and come join the living world. The weather's great over here.

I used to work with a church leadership team that was divided on the issue of hiring staff members versus enabling more volunteers to step up and take responsibility. Those who advocated hiring more paid staff argued that without compensation, no one would be willing to help on a consistent basis. The opposing view was that much of the work of the church should be done by volunteers anyway, and if you asked the right people to be responsible for specific, clearly defined tasks, the volunteers would work harder than someone who was paid.

You can probably guess that I fell on the side of those who advocated for volunteers. Personally, I think if you ask people to volunteer for a difficult mission, you'll get recruits with a much greater commitment than you could ever find otherwise. You may already be familiar with the classic "Shackleton" example used to illustrate this point. Ernest Shackleton, who led numerous expeditions to Antarctica in the early twentieth century, famously posted a recruitment flyer with the following statement:

> The ultimate measure of a man is not where he stands in moments of comfort and convenience, but where he stands at times of challenge and controversy.
>
> — MARTIN LUTHER KING JR.

Men wanted for Hazardous Journey. Small wages, bitter cold, long months of complete darkness, constant danger, safe return doubtful. Honour and recognition in case of success.

The advertisement was bold, daring, and also highly effective: Shackleton had plenty of problems with frostbite and running out of money, but he never had a serious problem recruiting sailors. After his "hazardous journey" flyer went out, more than

5,000 men applied for the job, which then involved getting stranded in the Antarctic for more than a year, subsisting on defrosted ice for water and clubbed seal for food.

You may not need to camp out on Antarctica and club your own dinner, but if you choose an unconventional journey of some kind, you'll probably end up feeling alone from time to time. Thankfully, you will also feel very alive. Many of us have found the feeling of being alive more than compensates for any negative consequences of living life on our own terms.

## A Few Dangerous Ideas

We've examined numerous dangerous ideas throughout the book. The belief that career security can be found internally rather than through a traditional job is highly dangerous. The fact that you can create a life based around what you love without being selfish is far from being widely accepted. The conventional model is still the myth of deferred gratification—spending the most productive years of our lives creating wealth that can only be enjoyed years or decades away in a distant future.

In fact, the basic belief that you should do what you want most of the time is uncomfortable and troubling for some people. So too is the conviction that our lives should count for much more than our own narrow interests. Before we charge out to storm the castle ("First we take Manhattan . . ."), let's look at a few other dangerous ideas that are worth spreading.

- Students could revolt and change universities, shifting the balance of power toward the group that enables the institution to exist in the first place. In no other institution in the world does a large majority willingly give over so much power to a tiny minority. Grading could be abolished or modified, and curriculums rewritten to reward trial and error more than rote memorization.

- Communities could abolish 98 percent of homelessness by allocating enough space for "tent cities" and free shelter for up to one year. (Despite numerous objections, this has been successfully implemented in several cities in Washington State and Quebec).

- Why should charities continue to exist after failing to solve the problems they were founded to address? If a business fails, it goes into bankruptcy and shuts its doors. Charities could solve problems and get out of the way.

- Prisons for non-violent offenders could be "open" centers where the occupants check in every day before going to a supervised job that contributes to society and helps them get back on track. (It's already being tried in Denmark and the Netherlands.)

- With enough commitment from individuals and groups, systemic poverty, malnutrition, and illiteracy could be completely eradicated within a few years *without* government funding.

Don't like these ideas? No problem—but what's *your* dangerous idea? The people who present, defend, and advance dangerous ideas will take personal responsibility. They will be dissatisfied with the status quo and will work hard to change it. While others stand back and complain, they will be the ones who make the world a better place.

## The Opposite of Luck

As we come to the end of our time together, I'd wish you good luck, but luck has very little to do with the rest of your journey. Luck, fate, childhood environment, social privilege—none of these things are completely irrelevant, but they aren't the whole story. A combination of factors has led us to become who we are today, and for better or worse, we cannot be completely responsible for our past.

What we *are* responsible for, however, is our future. What matters from here on out has little to do with luck and much more to do with our own choices. Let's look further at the quote from Sir Cecil Beaton used at the beginning of this chapter:

> Be daring, be different, be impractical, be anything that will assert integrity of purpose and imaginative vision against the play-it-safers, the creatures of the commonplace, the slaves of the ordinary.

**Be daring, be different.** In choosing to live a remarkable life, failure is a real possibility, but regrets are completely optional. If one plan doesn't work out, you can try something else—but if you never try, you'll go to your grave with your song still in you, as Henry David Thoreau wrote long ago.

**Be impractical.** You don't have to live your life the way other people expect you to. Most inventions were judged to be impractical at first glance. In the history of the world, provocative ideas that challenged authority were rarely welcomed by the people who controlled access to power and wealth.

**Assert integrity against the play-it-safers and slaves of the ordinary.** The world has enough sleepwalkers and cynics; the rest of us need your help. I've made a lot of mistakes along the path of my own unconventional journey. What I have refused to do is *settle*, and I hope you won't settle either.

Taking the road less traveled is a good start, but you can also build your own road. I hope to see you out there when our roads intersect, somewhere, sometime.

It's your turn now.

## POSTSCRIPT:
## THE MOST IMPORTANT THING

Someone once unsubscribed from my blog and left a note that said, "Thanks for everything, but I need to go it alone now." I don't like losing readers, but I instinctively understood what that person meant.

I hope you liked the book and I'd love to be a small part of your life somehow (a few options are in the next few pages), but if you have to choose between that and doing something great with your life, it's time for us to say goodbye.

It's far easier to be a cynic than a believer. Whatever you decide, don't do that. Stand for something! Come join the living world. The rest of us are waiting.

## GRATITUDE

Freedom is my highest personal value, but I try to keep gratitude a close second. Seth Godin and his Alternative MBA students helped me figure out that the best title for the book was probably the obvious one. Seth also regularly teaches me (and the rest of the world) about challenging the status quo and refusing to settle for mediocrity.

Pell grants from the U.S. Department of Education and a college fund from my dad helped fund five quarters of simultaneous enrollment at several colleges from 1995 to 1997. Thanks, President Clinton, and thanks, Dad.

No one is self-taught, and unconventional ideas do not usually arrive independently. I've been thinking about scarcity and abundance for a while, but while I was writing chapter 9, Chris Anderson published a whole book about it. (I was hoping it would be bad so I could ignore it, but it's actually quite good.) Similarly, Chris Brogan and Julien Smith wrote about building an army in their helpful book *Trust Agents*.

My personal heroes, Gary and Susan Parker, along with their

children Carys and Wesley, have lived in West Africa for 20 years and counting. While I drink cappuccinos in various countries around the world, they hang out in war zones and bring help to those who need it most. I think of them wherever I am, and hope that I can have 10 percent as much impact on the universe as they have.

A few people took a chance on me at important crossroads of life. Without their intervention (and willingness to stand up to others who said I wasn't ready), the course of my life would be much different. This group includes Daslin Small, Solfrid Quist, and whoever was on the University of Washington admissions committee that accepted me without GRE scores.

I am especially grateful to several people who have been part of my life at significant moments or were otherwise deeply influential to me. My enormous appreciation in this regard goes to Ken Dauer, Mary Guillebeau, Patricia Guillebeau, Regina Petersen, J. D. Roth, Kiana Swearingen, and Stephanie Zito.

David Fugate is my literary agent, but his role went much further than merely selling a book proposal. David cared about what I had to say before a lot of other people paid attention, and he spent a great deal of time improving the early drafts of the proposal.

Thanks to Maria Gagliano, rockstar editor, and everyone else at the Penguin Group for their handling and promotion of the book.

Superstar designer Reese Spykerman, specialist in branding and magic, has given a great deal of time and energy to helping me over the past two years. Whatever success I've had thus far is directly related to her generosity and skill.

Thanks to my colleagues in the LifeRemix network, and to Pamela Slim for setting a good example for me to follow.

Thanks to Scott Harrison and everyone at Charity: Water for a great partnership.

Huge thanks to everyone who reads the *Art of Non-Conformity* blog, especially those who have shared their feedback at different stages along the way. Thank you for making the site, and hopefully this book, much better than it would have been on my own. I'd love to blame vampires for any mistakes and shortcomings, but sadly, those are my own responsibility.

The most important expression of gratitude goes to Jolie Guillebeau, my partner in world domination and life. Jolie helped to improve the manuscript in several important ways, but mostly she continuously helps to improve my life in more ways than I could possibly count.

Fellow entrepreneurs, artists, travelers, and ass-kickers of the world, thank you for caring. If you've made it this far, I hope you found it worth your while. Feel free to let me know by writing in from ChrisGuillebeau.com.

Keep rocking the universe,

CHRIS GUILLEBEAU
PORTLAND, OREGON

## PARTNERSHIP WITH CHARITY: WATER AND ETHIOPIA

Most people in poor countries don't need a handout, but they do need help in changing their environment to increase their ability to make their own choices. Improving access to clean water and sanitation, something most of us take for granted every day, is a great start. I've partnered with my friends at Charity: Water to bring measurable, positive impact to communities around the world, starting with two areas in rural Ethiopia.

### How It Works

I will donate 20 percent of all royalties earned from sales of this book to the AONC partner project with Charity: Water for at least 12 months following publication. For each reader I meet who purchases the book during the Unconventional Book Tour or World Domination Summit events, I will donate an additional 80 percent of my royalties, for a total of 100 percent.

In an attempt to meet as many readers as possible, through-out the end of 2010 and beginning of 2011 I'll visit every state in the United States and every province in Canada (63 stops in all!). In the summer of 2011, I'll host a three-day event in Portland, Oregon, together with other speakers and fun people. For updates on the Unconventional Book Tour and the World Domination Summit, check out my site.

After the book tour and live event in Portland, I'll take a small group to visit Ethiopia and document the improvements that have been made as a result of the Charity: Water project. If you'd like to participate in any of these activities, please visit CharityWater.org/aonc. I'd love to partner with you in support of this worthy goal.

## FREQUENTLY ASKED QUESTIONS

*Isn't non-conformity for the sake of rebelling just another form of conformity?*

It certainly *can* be, if you don't have a purpose for the rebellion. I think of non-conformity as an alternative to sleepwalking. Choosing to be different is partly about questioning authority and conventional assumptions, but also about embracing life as a joyful, meaningful experience.

*What if everyone becomes a non-conformist?*

Everyone beginning to question authority, pursue big goals, and focus on helping others is like world peace: a wonderful idea that isn't likely to come true anytime soon.

*Why all the emphasis on friends and enemies? (Can't we all just get along?)*

Someone said, "It's easy to be a critic, because critics have no skin in the game." I wish everyone well, including those who prefer a traditional life and aren't attracted to alternative ideas. The only people

I am opposed to are those who try to prevent others from making their own choices.

### How do you travel everywhere and how much does it cost?

I use round-the-world tickets, a big stash of frequent flyer miles, and other kinds of travel hacking to get to almost anywhere in the world. My average flight cost is just under $400, including many long-haul flights to Asia, Europe, and Africa. The overall yearly cost is currently around $10,000 to $20,000, but keep in mind I go to a lot of hard-to-reach countries. Frequent travel to all kinds of interesting places can be done for much less if you don't need to make as many stops as I do.

### What do you think about sustainable tourism and the environmental impact of world travel?

I am in favor of sustainable tourism, and I see the choice between travel and sustainability as a false dichotomy. In the case of world travel, surely there is a way to be environmentally conscious without staying home all the time.

### What should I do with my life?

Something excellent that you want to do more than anything else in the world. When you start waking up at night with ideas, that's a good start.

### I can't decide about going to college (or university, or graduate school). What should I do?

I like what Bob Dylan said: "Colleges are like old-age homes, except for the fact that more people die in colleges." Whether it's college, university, graduate school, or something else, make sure you're doing it for your purposes instead of someone else's. This doesn't mean you shouldn't go—once I accepted the fact that 80 percent of it was a waste of time, I enjoyed my experience with higher education.

### To start a business, don't I need to raise a lot of money and go to business school?

You can start most businesses for less than $1,000, and many for less than $100. To get started, read Pamela Slim's *Escape from Cubicle Nation*, which at about $18 is a better investment than most classes you could take for much more money.

### How can I find out more and get involved?

I'd love to connect with you on my website, ChrisGuillebeau.com. I write at least 100 free articles a year and meet with people wherever I go in the world. Feel free to write me from the site and say hi.

## ONLINE RESOURCES

A few things didn't make it into the final version of this book. For the much-needed condensing, you can thank my editor Maria, who kept asking, "Does this need to be here? Can you get it out some other way?"

It was a good question, so I made a resources page on my website for everything that didn't make it in here. Among other things, the resources page includes:

- An introduction to travel hacking, including how to earn frequent flyer miles without flying, how to stay for free anywhere in the world, and where you can buy a round-the-world plane ticket

- A worksheet and MP3 audio download on creating the ideal day discussed in chapter 2

- More information on low-budget businesses, including a list of 10 ways to earn money through travel, and 10 businesses you can start for less than $100

- More help on building a small army using the "weak ties" phenomenon discussed in chapter 7

- A list of every person mentioned in the book, including everyone's website and contact info on Twitter and Facebook

All of this information is free, and you don't need to register to receive it. Just go to ChrisGuillebeau.com/book for a complete list.

## ABOUT THE AUTHOR

**Chris Guillebeau** travels the world and writes for a small army of remarkable people. From 2002 to 2006, he served as a volunteer for a medical charity in West Africa. After returning to the United States in 2006 and entering graduate school at the University of Washington, Chris began actively visiting countries like Burma, Uganda, Iraq, and Pakistan. On his personal quest to visit every country in the world, Chris has currently made it to 125 countries (only 67 to go!). He is a regular contributor to CNN.com, *Business Week*, *Huffington Post*, and other outlets. When not roaming elsewhere, Chris lives in Portland, Oregon.